The Use and Abuse of Biology

The Use and Abuse of Biology

An Anthropological Critique of Sociobiology

Marshall Sahlins

TAVISTOCK PUBLICATIONS

First published in Great Britain in 1977
by Tavistock Publications Limited
11 New Fetter Lane, London EC4P 4EE
Printed in Great Britain by photolithography
at the University Press, Cambridge

ISBN 0 422 76270 9

I always like to [tell] a story Wundt's assistant, Külpe, told us after a visit to the neighboring University of Jena to see the aged philosopher Erdmann, whose history of philosophy, in some ten volumes, we had all read and studied. They had a warm, friendly talk, the old scholar and the young scientist, all about the old philosophers and their systems. But when Külpe tried to draw him out on Wundt and the newer school, Erdmann shook his head, declaring that he could not understand the modern men. "In my day," he explained, "we used to ask the everlasting question: What is man?': And you—nowadays you answer it, saying, 'he *was* an ape.'"

LINCOLN STEFFANS, *The Autobiography*

Contents

Introduction

The publication of Edward O. Wilson's *Sociobiology:
The New Synthesis* in the fall of 1975 was greeted,
both within and beyond the academy, with a response of historic proportions. At least the reaction
was all out of the proportions usually accorded a
scholarly work issued by a scholarly press. Actually
the storm had been building for years: Mr. Wilson,
as he would readily acknowledge, is not the first
sociobiologist, although he is clearly the most effective and comprehensive. The book in any case
became a "media event," subject of feature stories
and even front-page headlines in the *New York
Times*, the *Chicago Tribune*, and other leading
American dailies. It set off a running debate, as yet
without resolution, in the pages of the *New York
Review of Books* and in *Science*, the journal of the
American Association for the Advancement of Science. By the spring of 1976, lectures and entire
courses, pro and con, were being offered on the new
discipline of sociobiology at Harvard, the University
of Chicago, the University of Michigan, and other
distinguished places of higher learning. A critical
attack, issued by the Boston-based collective "Science for the People," was being vended at advanced
intellectual kiosks across the country. The American
Anthropological Association reserved two days of

symposia on the subject at its annual meetings in November, 1976, at which Wilson as well as other biologists and sympathetic anthropologists would argue the case for a major redirection in social-science thinking. In brief, *Sociobiology* has occasioned a crisis of *connaissance* and *conscience*, of knowledge and public consciousness, with overtones as much political or ideological as they have been academic. Willy-nilly, the present essay becomes part of the controversy. It addresses the general intellectual and ideological issues raised by *Sociobiology* and related writings from the particular vantage of a practicing anthropologist, which is to say, from a traditional vantage of what *culture* is. The tenor will be critical but I hope not hysterical.

For the central intellectual problem does come down to the autonomy of culture and of the study of culture. *Sociobiology* challenges the integrity of culture as a thing-in-itself, as a distinctive and symbolic human creation. In place of a social constitution of meanings, it offers a biological determination of human interactions with a source primarily in the general evolutionary propensity of individual genotypes to maximize their reproductive success. It is a new variety of sociological utilitarianism, but transposed now to a biological calculus of the utilities realized in social relations. As a corollary, sociobiologists propose to change the face and structure of the human disciplines. The "New Synthesis" is to include the humanities and social sciences. As the subject matter of these disciplines is not truly unique, they should be incorporated within an evolutionary biology that is prepared to supply their fundamental determinations. "Sociology and the other social sciences," E. O. Wilson writes, "as well as the humanities, are the last branches of biology waiting to be included in the Modern Synthesis. One of the functions of sociobiology, then, is to reformulate the foundations of the social sciences in a way that draws these subjects into the Modern Synthesis. Whether the social sciences can be truly biologicized in this fashion remains to be seen" (1975, p. 4).

The answer I suggest here is that they cannot, because biology, while it is an absolutely necessary condition for culture, is equally and absolutely insufficient: it is completely unable to specify the cultural properties of human behavior or their variations from one human group to another.

The political problems posed by the publication of *Sociobiology* have developed both inside the academy and in the society at large. As for the first, I will say nothing at length. It is only worth noting that the project of encompassment of other disciplines has become practice as well as theory. Anthropologists, sociologists, and others who have been convinced of the correctness of the sociobiological thesis find in it also a means of organized interdisciplinary competition. Sometimes the aggressiveness of the "attack" on the traditional wisdom—for so it has been characterized to me by an anthropologist *cum* sociobiologist—seems designed to describe and prove their theory of human nature at one and the same time.

On the other hand, in the larger society sociobiologists have had to bear vigorous attacks from people of the Left. Most of the discussion in the newspapers and intellectual journals is of this type. Although the practitioners of sociobiology are as bound to their ivory towers as any of us, which is to say that the only politics they know very well are rather of the feudal variety, they suddenly find

themselves victimized (as they see it) as archde-
fenders of a conservative capitalism. Sociobiology is
denounced as another incarnation of social Darwinism. The sociobiologists are accused of perpe-
trating an ideological justification for an oppressive
status quo in which they happen to be rather privileged participants. (For a recent version of the debate, see *Bio Science*, March, 1976.) I do not think
that Wilson and his coworkers were prepared for
this kind of ideological reaction. Some might say
that they were unaware of the political dimensions
of their argument, but this poses complex issues of
criticism which again are presented on two levels.

The first is, what to say about the intentions of
the sociobiologists, or more precisely, are their motivations at all relevant? I would say they are not at
all relevant, and I should like to refrain from the
slightest suggestion of *ad hominem* criticism. This
for a principled reason which happens to be one of
my main criticisms of the theory itself; namely, that
there is no necessary relation between the cultural
character of a given act, institution, or belief and the
motivations people may have for participating in it.
While I do believe that the theory of sociobiology
has an intrinsic ideological dimension, in fact a pro-
found historical relation to Western competitive
capitalism, this itself is a fact that has to be culturally
and meaningfully analyzed—precisely because the
lack of agreement between the character of the
ideological act and the quality of the intent precludes
any easy individualistic explanation.

Furthermore, and this is the second difficulty
which criticism must acknowledge, it can be argued
that there is no logical isomorphism either between
sociobiology and social oppression. In a recent interview in the *Harvard Crimson*, E. O. Wilson is re-

ported to have pointed out that, after all, Noam Chomsky is an "innatist" too—and surely Chomsky is a politically honorable man. But if, the argument runs, we insist scientifically on the infinite plasticity and malleability of human behavior, ignoring the biological constraints on human thought and action, that too is an open invitation to any tinhorn totalitarian to do with us what he will. And we will get no better than what we should. Now while this argument is surely discussable, I should like to concede the point, because again the lack of any strictly rational connection between the innatist outlook and social iniquity could sharpen the cultural dimensions of the issue. How, then, are we to explain the sensitivity of the Left to the thesis of sociobiology? For that sensitivity is surely a social fact. And how are we to account for the fascination of the public and the media? That is another social fact. The ideological controversy provoked by sociobiology is an important cultural phenomenon in itself. It suggests some kind of deep relation between the theory of human action advanced by sociobiology and the self-consciousness Westerners have of their own social existence. There is some relation here between the biological model of the animal kingdom and the natives' model of themselves. Now if the natives concerned were of some other tribe, the anthropologist would without hesitation think it his task to try to discover that relation. Yet if there is culture anywhere in humanity, there is culture even in America, and no less obligation on the anthropologist's part to consider it as such, though he find it even more difficult to work as an observing participant than as a participant observer. I should like to treat the ideological issues in this kind of ethnographic spirit.

Part 1, Biology and Culture, attempts to determine the inadequacies of sociobiology as a theory of culture. It consists of a critique in two stages. The first will be a brief criticism of what I call "the vulgar sociobiology," which is not so much the work of Wilson as a premise taken up by the New Synthesis from certain recent predecessors. The premise is that human social phenomena are the direct expression of human behavioral dispositions or emotions, such as aggressiveness, sexuality, or altruism, the dispositions themselves having been laid down in the course of mammalian, primate, or hominid phylogeny. The next and longer section is concerned with "kin selection," which is a particularly salient form of the idea that human social behavior is determined by a calculus of individual reproductive success; that is, that all kinds of sociability and asociability can be explained by the evolutionary tendency of the genetic material to maximize itself over time. The objection to this view constitutes a critique of "the scientific sociobiology" represented by Wilson and colleagues.

Part 2, Biology and Ideology, examines the transformations of evolutionary theory itself that have been occasioned by its ventures into social organization, especially human social organization. I argue that the traditional understanding of "natural selection" has been progressively assimilated to the theory of social action characteristic of the competitive marketplace, theory characteristic of a late and historically specific development of Euro-American culture. From the idea of differential reproduction dependent on chance genetic and environmental shifts, selection successively became synonymous with optimization or maximization of individual genotypes, and ultimately with the exploitation of one organism by another in the interest of an egotistical genetic fitness. In the course of this series of transformations, selection surrenders its theoretical position as the orienting force of evolution in favor of the genetic maximization project of the individual subject. In the structure of evolutionary argumentation, selection takes the role of a means of the organism's ends. A second section traces the parallel development in the sociological and popular self-consciousness of Western civilization itself. Ever since Hobbes placed the bourgeois society he knew in the state of nature, the ideology of capitalism has been marked by a reciprocal dialectic between the folk conceptions of culture and nature. Conceived in the image of the market system, the nature thus culturally figured has been in turn used to explain the human social order, and vice versa, in an endless reciprocal interchange between social Darwinism and natural capitalism. Sociobiology, it is argued, is only the latest phase in this cycle: the grounding of human social behavior in an advanced or scientific notion of organic evolution, which is in its own terms the representation of a cultural form of economic action. Hence, we have the popular and political reaction that greeted the announcement of this "New Synthesis."

It remains to note that I have written this essay with some sense of urgency, given the current significance of sociobiology, and the good possibility that it will soon disappear as science, only to be preserved in a renewed popular conviction of the naturalness of our cultural dispositions. For this reason the usual scholarly apparatus of extensive footnotes has been dispensed with. Key references are given in the text and the few footnotes explicate technical terms—which I have generally tried to keep to a minimum.

Part One

Biology and Culture

I

Critique of the Vulgar Sociobiology

> "They're trying to kill me," Yossarian told him calmly.
>
> "No one's trying to kill you," Clevinger cried.
>
> "Then why are they shooting at me?" Yossarian asked.
>
> "They're shooting at *everyone*," Clevinger answered. "They're trying to kill everyone."
>
> "And what difference does that make?" . . .
>
> "Who's they?" he wanted to know. "Who, specifically, do you think is trying to murder you?"
>
> "Every one of them," Yossarian told him.
>
> "Every one of whom?"
>
> "Every one of whom do you think?"
>
> "I haven't any idea."
>
> "Then how do you know they aren't?"
>
> JOSEPH HELLER, *Catch 22*

Taken generally, the vulgar sociobiology consists in the explication of human social behavior as the expression of the needs and drives of the human organism, such propensities having been constructed in human nature by biological evolution.

Anthropologists will recognize the close parallel to the "functionalism" of Malinowski, who like-

3

wise tried to account for cultural phenomena by the biological needs they satisfied. It has been said that for Malinowski culture was a gigantic metaphorical extension of the physiological processes of digestion.

It would take more effort, however, to recognize the thesis of vulgar sociobiology in the works of scientific biologists such as E. O. Wilson, R. L. Trivers, W. D. Hamilton, R. Alexander, or M. West-Eberhard. These scholars have not been concerned as such to make the case that human social organization represents natural human dispositions. That thesis has been the preoccupation of authors of the recent past, proponents of a less rigorous biological determinism, such as Ardrey, Lorenz, Morris, Tiger, and Fox. Scientific sociobiology is distinguished by a more rigorous and comprehensive attempt to place social behavior on sound evolutionary principles, notably the principle of the self-maximization of the individual genotype, taken as the fundamental logic of natural selection. Yet by the nature of that attempt, the main proposition of the vulgar sociobiology becomes also the necessary premise of a scientific sociobiology. The latter merely anchors the former in genetic-evolutionary processes. The chain of biological causation is accordingly lengthened: from genes through phenotypical dispositions to characteristic social interactions. But the idea of a necessary correspondence between the last two, between human emotions or needs and human social relations, remains indispensable to the scientific analysis.

The position of the vulgar sociobiology is that innate human drives and dispositions, such as aggressiveness or altruism, male "bonding," sexuality of a certain kind or a parental interest in one's off-

spring, are realized in social institutions of a corresponding character. The interaction of organisms
will inscribe these organic tendencies in their social
relations. Accordingly, there is a one-to-one parallel
between the character of human biological propensities and the properties of human social systems.
Corresponding to human aggressiveness we find
among all men a taste for violence and warfare, as
well as territoriality and systems of social ranking
or dominance. Marriage, adultery, harlotry, and
(male) promiscuity may be understood as expressions of a bisexual and highly sexual species. A long
period of infant dependency finds its cultural analogue in universal norms of motherhood and fatherhood. Note that this kind of reasoning is also im-
plicitly, explicitly, and extensively adopted by Wilson
and his coworkers. *Sociobiology* opens with a discussion of the critical relevance of the hypothalmic
and limbic centers of the human brain, as evolved
by natural selection, to the formulation of any ethi-
cal or moral philosophy. These centers are said to
"flood our consciousness with emotions" and to
"orchestrate our behavioral responses" in such a way
as to maximally proliferate the responsible genes.
But most generally the thesis of the vulgar sociobiology is built into the scientific sociobiologist's
idea of social organization. For him, any Durkheim-
ian notion of the independent existence and persistence of the social fact is a lapse into mysticism.
Social organization is rather, and nothing more
than, the behavioral outcome of the interaction of
organisms having biologically fixed inclinations.
There is nothing in society that was not first in the
organisms. The ensuing system of statuses and
structures is a function of demography and disposition, of the distribution in the group of animals of

different age, sex, or other classes, each with its characteristic behavioral propensities. Therefore, we can always resolve the empirical social forms into the behavioral inclinations of the organisms in question, and that resolution will be exhaustive and comprehensive. The idea I want to convey is one of isomorphism between the biological properties and the social properties.

Related to this premise of isomorphism is a mode of discourse characteristic of vulgar sociobiology, which amounts to a nomenclature or classification of social behavior. I refer to the famous temptations of anthropomorphism. Observing animal social relations and statuses, we recognize in them certain similarities to human institutions: as between territorial competition and human warfare, animal dominance and human rank or class, mating and marriage, and so forth. The analogy, the argument runs, is often indeed a functional homology; that is, it is based on common genetic capacities and phylogenetic continuities, an evolutionary identity of the dispositional underpinning. It follows that the social behaviors in question, human and nonhuman alike, deserve the same designation, which is to say that they belong in the same class of social relations. Usually the English name for the animal activity is taken as the general (or unmarked) label of the class, such that war is subsumed in "territoriality" or chieftainship in "dominance." Sometimes, however, the marked or anthropological term is adopted as the general name for the class and applied also to the animal counterparts. This, of course, smuggles in certain important propositions about the "culture" of animals. Again the anthropomorphic inclination is not confined to the vulgar sociobiology. To take a random and limited sample from Wilson's *Sociobiology: The New Synthesis*, we read of animal societies that have "polygyny," "castes," "slaves," "despots," "matrilineal social organization," "aunts," "queens," "family chauvinism," "culture," "cultural innovation," "agriculture," "taxes," and "investments," as well as "costs" and "benefits."

I shall not be concerned with this anthropomorphic taxonomy, which has been justly and effectively criticized by many others, so much as with the essential anthropological problem in the thesis of vulgar sociobiology. It is a problem that has often recurred in the history of anthropological thought, not only with Malinowski but principally in the "personality and culture" school of the 1940s and 1950s. The inability to resolve the problem in favor of psychological explanations of culture accounts for the more modest aims of that school at present, as well as for the change of name to "psychological anthropology." The problem is that there is no necessary relation between the phenomenal form of a human social institution and the individual motivations that may be realized or satisfied therein. The idea of a fixed correspondence between innate human dispositions and human social forms constitutes a weak link, a rupture in fact, in the chain of sociobiological reasoning.

Let me explain first by a very simple example, a matter of commonplace observation. Consider the relation between warfare and human aggression— what Wilson at one point calls "the true, biological joy of warfare." It is evident that the people engaged in fighting wars—or for that matter, any kind of fighting—are by no means necessarily aggressive, either in the course of action or beforehand. Many are plainly terrified. People engaged in wars may have any number of motivations to do so, and typically these stand in some contrast to a simple behaviorist characterization of the event as "violence." Men may be moved to fight out of love (as of country) or humaneness (in light of the brutality attributed to the enemy), for honor or some sort of self-esteem, from feelings of guilt, or to save the world for democracy. It is a priori difficult to conceive—and a fortiori even more difficult for an anthropologist to conceive—of any human disposition that cannot be satisfied by war, or more correctly, that cannot be socially mobilized for its prosecution. Compassion, hate, generosity, shame, prestige, emulation, fear, contempt, envy, greed—ethnographically the energies that move men to fight are practically coterminous with the range of human motivations. And that by virtue of another commonplace of anthropological and ordinary experience: that the reasons people fight are not the reasons wars take place.

If the reasons why millions of Americans fought in World War II were laid end to end, they would not account for the occurrence or the nature of that war. No more than from the mere fact of their fighting could one understand their reasons. For war is not a relation between individuals but between states (or other socially constituted polities), and people participate in them not in their capacities as individuals or as human beings but as social beings—and indeed not exactly that, but only in a specifically contextualized social capacity. "They're trying to kill me," Yossarian told him calmly. "No one's trying to kill you." "Then why are they shooting at me?" Yossarian might have had some relief from the answer of a Rousseau rather than a Clevinger. In a stunning passage of the *Social Contract*, Rousseau justifies the title some would give him as the true ancestor of anthropology by arguing the status of war as a phenomenon of *cultural* nature —precisely against the Hobbesian view of a war of every man against every man grounded in human nature. "War," Rousseau wrote, "is not a relation between man and man, but between State and State, and *individuals are enemies accidentally, not as men, nor even as citizens, but as soldiers;* not as members of their country but as its defenders. Finally, each State can have for enemies only other States, and not men; for between things disparate in nature there can be no real relation" (italics added).

The general point is that human needs and dispositions are not just realized, fulfilled, or expressed in war; they are mobilized. It is certain that a capacity for aggression can be, and often is, symbolically trained and unleashed. But aggression need not be present at all in a man bombing an unseen target in the jungle from a height of 25,000 feet, even as it is always so contingent on the cultural context that, as in the case of the ancient Hawaiians, an army of thousands, upon seeing one of their members successfully dragged off as a sacrifice to the enemy's gods, will suddenly drop its weapons and fly to the mountains. Aggression does not regulate social conflict, but social conflict does regulate aggression. Moreover, any number of different needs may be thus engaged, exactly because satisfaction does not depend on the formal character of the institution but on the meaning attributed to it. For men, emotions are symbolically orchestrated and fulfilled in social actions. As for the actions themselves, as social facts their appropriateness does not lie in their correspondence to human dispositions but in their relations to the cultural context: as an act of war is related to an international power structure, godless Communism, insolent nationalism, diminishing capital funds, and the national distribution of oil.

Is violence an act of aggression, generosity a sign of "altruism"? Ethnographers of Melanesia as well as psychoanalysts of America will readily testify that aggression is often satisfied by making large and unrequited gifts. For as the Eskimo also say, "Gifts make slaves, as whips make dogs." On the other hand, a person may well hit another out of a true concern for the latter's welfare. One man's altruism becomes some child's sore behind; and, "Believe me, I'm doing this for your own good. It hurts me more than it hurts you." There is, in human affairs, a motivational arbitrariness of the social sign that runs parallel to, in fact is due to, Saussure's famous referential arbitrariness of the linguistic sign. Any given psychological disposition is able to take on an indefinite set of institutional realizations. We war on the playing fields of Ann Arbor, express sexuality by painting a picture, even indulge our aggressions and commit mayhem by writing books and giving lectures. Conversely, it is impossible to say in advance what needs may be realized by any given social activity. That is why Ruth Benedict, upon examining diverse patterns of culture, came to the conclusion that one cannot define a given social domain by a characteristic human motive, such as economics by the drive to accumulate wealth or politics by the quest for power. The act of exchange? It may well find inspiration in a hedonistic greed, but just as well in pity, aggression, dominance, love, honor, or duty.

"Pleasure" (or "satisfaction," or "utility") is not a natural phenomenon like the "five senses" of the physical organism. For every man it is determined by the social medium in which he lives; and consequently when it is adopted as a tool of analysis or a term of explanation of that social order, its adoption means the assumption in advance of all that social fabric of which an explanation is being sought. We hold this truth to be self-evident, that men who live by democracy, or by capital, will find in it their happiness, and that is all that is self-evident (Ayres 1944, p. 75).

In sum, the sociobiological reasoning from evolutionary phylogeny to social morphology is interrupted by culture. One could be persuaded to accept the more dubious or unproved assertions at the base of this logical chain; for example, that human emotional dispositions are genetically controlled and that the genetic controls were sedimented by adaptive processes at a time beyond memory. It still would not follow that the constraints of the biological base "orchestrate our behavioral responses" and account thereby for the present social arrangements of men. For between the basic drives that may be attributed to human nature and the social structures of human culture there enters a critical indeterminacy. The same human motives appear in different cultural forms, and different motives appear in the same forms. A fixed correspondence being lacking between the character of society and the human character, there can be no biological determinism.

Culture is the essential condition of this freedom of the human order from emotional or motivational necessity. Men interact in the terms of a system of meanings, attributed to persons and the objects of their existence, but precisely as these attributes are symbolic they cannot be discovered in the intrinsic properties of the things to which they refer. The process rather is one of valuation of certain "objective" properties. An animal stands as an ancestor, and even so the son of a man's brother may be one of the clan of the ancestor's descendants while the son of his sister is an outsider, and perhaps, an enemy. Yet if matrilineal descent were deemed salient, all this would be reversed and the sister's son not a stranger but one's own proper heir. For the inhabitants of a Polynesian island, the sea is a "higher" social element than the land and the trade winds blowing from east to west likewise are conceived to proceed from "above" to "below." Accordingly, a house is oriented with its sacred sides toward the east and toward the sea, and only men who are of the appropriate chiefly descent should build these sides, which once finished will be the domestic domain of a man and his senior sons, who relative to the women of the family are "chiefly." By the same token, only the men will fish on the deep sea or cultivate in the higher land; whereas, their women work exclusively in the village and inside the reef, that is, the land side of the sea. The social arrangements are constructed on a meaningful logic, which in fact constitutes a human world out of an "objective" one which can offer to the former a variety of possible distinctions but no necessary significations. Thus, while the human world depends on the senses, and the whole panoply of organic characteristics supplied by biological evolution, its freedom from biology consists in just the capacity to give these their own sense.

In the symbolic event, a radical discontinuity is introduced between culture and nature. The isomorphism between the two required by the sociobiological thesis does not exist. The symbolic system of culture is not just an expression of human nature, but has a form and dynamic consistent with its properties as meaningful, which make it rather an intervention in nature. Culture is not ordered by the primitive emotions of the hypothalmus; it is the emotions which are organized by culture. We have not to deal, therefore, with a biological sequence of events proceeding from the genotype to the social type by way of a phenotype already programmed for social behavior by natural selection. The structure of determinations is a hierarchical one set the other way round: a meaningful system of the world and human experience that was already in existence before any of the current human participants were born, and that from birth engages their natural dispositions as the instruments of a symbolic project. If thus necessary to the symbolic function, these dispositions are in the same measure insufficient to an anthropological explanation since they cannot specify the cultural content of any human social order.

(The proposition that human emotions are culturally constituted, although here stated synchronically, as a recurrent fact of social life could also be extended phylogenetically. As Clifford Geertz [1973] has so effectively argued, to say that a given human disposition is "innate" is not to deny that it was also culturally produced. The biology of mankind has been shaped by culture, which is itself considerably older than the human species as we know it. Culture was developed in the hominid line about three million years ago. The modern species of man, *Homo sapiens*, originated and gained ascendancy about one hundred thousand years ago. It is reasonable to suppose that the dispositions we observe in modern man, and notably the capacity—indeed, the necessity—to organize and define these dispositions symbolically, are effects of a prolonged cultural selection. "Not only ideas," Geertz writes, "but emotions too, are cultural artifacts in man" [ibid., p. 81]. When the full implications of this simple but powerful argument are finally drawn, a great deal of what passes today for the biological "basis" of human behavior will be better understood as the cultural mediation of the organism.)

We can see now that the theoretical demand of sociobiology for an isomorphism of behavioral traits and social relations requires an empirical procedure that is equally erroneous. Sociobiology is compelled to take a naive behaviorist view of human social acts. Observing warfare, the sociobiologist concludes he is in the presence of an underlying aggression. Seeing an act of food sharing, he knows it as a disposition toward altruism. For him, the appearance of a social fact is the same thing as its motivation; he immediately places the first within a category of the second. Yet the understanding must remain as superficial as the method, since for people, these are not simply acts but meaningful acts. As for the acts, their cultural reasons for being lie elsewhere, even as the participants' reasons for doing may betray all the appearances.

By a roundabout way we thus return to the true issue in anthropomorphic terminology, for the error in metaphorically assimilating cultural forms to animal behaviors is the same as is involved in translating the contents of social relations in terms of their motivations. Both are procedures of what Sartre (1963) calls "the terror." Sartre applies the phrase to "vulgar Marxist" reductions of superstructural facts to infrastructural determinations, art for example to economics, such that Valéry's poetry becomes "a species of bourgeois idealism"; but it will do as well for the analogous reductions to the human species favored by the vulgar sociobiology. To speak of World War II, the sporadic combats between Australian bands or New Guinea head-hunting as acts of aggression or territoriality is like-wise an "inflexible refusal to differentiate," a pro-gram of elimination whose aim is "total assimilation at the least possible cost." In a similar way, it dissolves the autonomous and variable cultural con-tents beyond all hope of recovering them. The method consists of taking the concrete properties of an act, such as war, the actual character of World War II or Vietnam, as merely an ostensible appear-ance. The real truth of such events lies elsewhere; essentially, they are "aggression." But note that in so doing, one provides causes—"aggression," "sex-uality," "egotism," etc.—which themselves have the appearance of being basic and fundamental but are in reality abstract and indeterminate. Meanwhile, in this resolution of the concrete instance to an abstract reason, everything distinctively cultural about the act has been allowed to escape. We can never get back to its empirical specifications—who actually fights whom, where, when, how, and why—because all these properties have been dissolved in the biological characterization. It is, as Sartre says, "a bath of sul-phuric acid." To attribute any or all human wars, dominance hierarchies, or the like to human aggres-siveness is a kind of bargain made with reality in which an understanding of the phenomenon is gained at the cost of everything we know about it. We have to suspend our comprehension of what it is. But a theory ought to be judged as much by the ignorance it demands as by the knowledge it purports to afford. Between "aggression" and Vietnam, "sexuality" and cross-cousin marriage, "reciprocal altruism" and the exchange rate of red shell necklaces, biology offers us merely an enormous intellectual void. Its place can be filled only by a theory of the nature and dynamics of culture as a meaningful system. Within the void left by biology lies the whole of anthropology.

II
Critique of the Scientific Sociobiology: Kin Selection

What keeps a man alive?
He lives on others:
He likes to taste them first,
Then eat them whole if he can;
Forgets that they're supposed to be his brothers,
That he himself was ever called a man.

Remember if you wish to stay alive,
For once do something bad
And you'll survive!

BERTOLT BRECHT, *Three Penny Opera*

Whether the scientific sociobiology will succeed in its ambition of incorporating the human sciences depends largely on the fate of its theory of kin selection. This is true for several reasons. One is the significance of kinship in the so-called primitive societies, from which may be inferred its importance throughout the earlier and greater portion of human history. Sociobiology purports to provide a theory of that importance and of how kinship behavior is ordered. E. O. Wilson suggests that, "the

17

extent and formalization of kinship prevailing in almost all human societies are . . . unique features of the biology of our species" (1975, p. 554). On the second part of the statement most anthropologists will take issue. They have passed decades arguing that kinship is no more "biological" in any human society than in the stipulation of the Napoleonic Code that the father of the child is the husband of the mother. On the first part of the statement, however, there is agreement, and so an arena for discussion. Kinship is the dominant structure of many of the peoples anthropologists have studied, the prevailing code not only in the domestic sphere but generally of economic, political, and ritual action. The problem is whether this fact is cultural or, as Wilson says, biological; and, whether the explanation ought to at least include biological factors. But there is still another issue which makes the problem doubly critical. It is that the interpretation sociobiology offers for kinship is only a special instance of its reliance on the idea of individual reproductive success as the mainspring of social behavior—not only in men but throughout the animal kingdom. This emphasis is a logical deduction from the definition of natural selection as differential reproduction among members of a species or population. An effective anthropological criticism of kin selection, therefore, would do great damage to the thesis and interdisciplinary objectives of sociobiology. If kinship is not ordered by individual reproductive success, and if kinship is admittedly central to human social behavior, then the project of an encompassing sociobiology collapses. The issue between sociobiology and social anthropology is decisively joined on the field of kinship.

Sociobiology, however, has had its own internal

reasons for according an unusual significance to kinship. Its attention to this field was not motivated in the first place by ethnographic report, but developed within biology as part of a dialectical opposition to the theory of "group selection." In the perspective of group selection—the classic exemplar is Wynne-Edwards's *Animal Dispersion in Relation to Social Behaviour* (1962)—the unit of genetic response to environmental circumstance is the population of interbreeding organisms. The genetic pool of the population is the true subject of selective pressure and evolutionary change. But, ask the opponents of group selection, how can this be if genetic reproduction and change is exclusively the function of the individual organism? Selection must work fundamentally through the individual, as "individual selection." Paradox turns into contradiction when it becomes a question of explaining the persistence of certain "altruistic" behaviors, such as the raising of an alarm against attack which is likely to render the sentinel the first victim of predation, or actually giving one's life in defense of the hive or horde. The contradiction is that such self-sacrifice will be selected against individually. As the organism practicing it is vulnerable to an early death, the genes responsible for it would disappear from the population's stock. Yet it remains the empirical case that defense of the group at the risk to individual life is a propensity reproduced from generation to generation, that is, as a species-specific characteristic of certain birds and mammals as well as social insects. How then does one retrieve the basic understanding of selection as the differential reproduction of individual genotypes, from which it follows that every organism is essentially in egotistic competition with every other member of the group? Theoretically, selection would favor a self-interest in reproductive success at the cost of whom it may concern. "Every adaptation," an influential critic of group selection points out, "is calculated to maximize the reproductive success of the individual, relative to other individuals, regardless of what effect this maximization has on the population" (Williams 1966, p. 160). And from this follows the idea that the finality of DNA is self-maximization by means of the organism or its behavior. Incidentally, one sees here how a theoretical debate within biology can engage an ideological dialectic of the larger society. Opposing individual selection to group selection as egotism is different from altruism, biologists represent the scientific content of the first opposition as the folk concept of the second. As against the "altruism" of group selection, they figure individual selection in the terms of an economic metaphor of enterprising individualism.

The solution of the biological contradiction has been ingenious. As first developed by Hamilton under the name of "kin selection" (1964; 1970; 1972), and then elaborated by others (e.g., West-Eberhard 1975), it consists of transforming social altruism into genetic egotism by the observation that the "kin" of the self-sacrificing animal, who share a certain amount of genetic substance with him, are often benefited by his act. Therefore, service to others can actually optimize ego's "inclusive fitness," the proportion of his genes passed on to subsequent generations. This net advantage occurs in the measure that the benefit to the same genes as possessed by kinsmen is greater than the cost to one's own reproductive success. For sociobiologists, altruism is the spite of life.

Kin selection can be represented in a precise

mathematical formula of cost-benefit form. The original and essential formula as proposed by Hamilton is:

$$k > 1/\bar{r},$$

where

k = a factor of $\dfrac{\text{benefit to others' reproductive success}}{\text{cost to ego's reproductive success}}$

r = the coefficient of relationship, or average shared heredity between ego and a kinsman of a certain genealogical type,

and $\bar{r}$ = the average coefficient of relationship to the ensemble of relatives benefited.

So, for example, as I share on average 1/2 of my genetic substance with a brother, even suicide may increase my inclusive fitness, so long as the act saves from death more than two of my siblings. Likewise, if I could save more than eight of my first cousins, or provide some reproductive benefit to a first cousin more than eight times the cost to my own, the apparently altruistic service would actually be in my genetic self-interest (cf. Wilson 1975, pp. 117-20 et passim; the formulae for calculating r or "coefficient of relationship" are given on pp. 74 ff. For diploid species, as mammals, the usual rule of thumb is: multiply every collateral and/or lineal step in the shortest genealogical path between two kinsmen by a factor of 1/2).

It is important to note that this formula will not only account for altruism but also for a whole panoply of asocial or unsociable behaviors, such as selfishness or ingratitude, the refusal to share or otherwise show generosity to certain members of the group —even spiteful hostility, so long as the cost to one's own reproduction confers an advantage relative to the losses of others. Selection will favor any type of positive or negative social action that maintains k above $1/\bar{r}$, while penalizing any individual who does not have this kind of proper regard for his own reproductive success. This one simple formula amounts to a powerful, global logic of social behavior on the principle of utilitarian individualism —particularly, if paradoxically, in those "primitive" societies where individuality is embedded in an extensive system of kinship groups and relations. It is like Hobbes's "motion toward" and "motion away," appetite for one's own good and aversion to one's own evil (see below), comprehending thus the quasitotality of social intercourse on the premise of an enlightened self-concern. In this respect, sociobiology's plan for subordinating the social sciences and humanities within the positive science of evolutionary biology seems rather wasteful of academic efforts. The laws of rational action to which it aspires have already been mathematically refined and widely applied by the science of economics, especially the microeconomics. They have even been applied to social behaviors, such as marriage and divorce (cf. Schultz 1974). It would only be necessary to substitute genetic values for "utilities" in the formulations of the Chicago School of Economics. Actually, the "Modern Synthesis" has been around for at least two centuries.

Meanwhile, in order to participate in a dialogue with sociobiology, anthropologists will have to agree, if only momentarily, that kinship may be defined as "genealogical connections." They will have to suspend their hard-won understanding that human kinship is not a naturally given set of "blood relationships" but a culturally variable system of meaningful categories (cf. Schneider 1968; 1972). The concession is necessary because of the form that sociobiology's own argument has taken in the face of the apparent arbitrariness of kinship classifications, as well as the prevalence of moral codes that do not ostensibly conform to the rationality of genetic self-interest. The response of sociobiology is that knowledge of genealogical relationships is always the secret wisdom of the genes, whatever the apparent form of a people's consciousness. And as the calculus of egotistical action on this genealogical basis is selectively advantageous, it is at the least "intuitive" and manifest in de facto social effects, even if it is not expressly articulated as a moral principle. Presumably, the algebra of kin selection also will be unconscious. Thus, it does not matter what people—including ethnographers—may say or think; as biological organisms they are compelled by natural laws to maximize their inclusive fitness. Indeed it may be of adaptive value, insofar as group living confers any benefits, to mystify our natural selfishness under the cover of more generous cultural sentiments. "In terms of evolutionary history," writes R. D. Alexander, "human behavior tends to maximize the bearer's reproduction. Selection has probably worked against the understanding of such selfish motivations becoming a part of human consciousness, or perhaps being easily acceptable" (1975, p. 96). From this, incidentally, issues a view of social life more or less widely shared by sociobiologists: society is basically founded on lies. Human society, Alexander tells us, "is a network of lies and deception, persisting only because systems of conventions about permissable kinds and

extents of lying have arisen" (ibid.). In *Sociobiology*
E. O. Wilson frequently insinuates the same kind
of conception:

> . . . self-sacrifice on behalf of second cous-
> ins is true altruism [in both the conventional
> and genetic senses] . . . and when directed at
> total strangers such abnegating behavior is so
> surprising (that is "noble") as to demand some
> kind of theoretical explanation. In contrast, a
> person who raises his own fitness by lowering
> that of others is engaged in *selfishness*. While
> we cannot publicly approve the selfish act we
> do understand it thoroughly and may even sym-
> pathize. Finally, a person who gains nothing
> or even reduces his own fitness in order to
> diminish that of another has committed an act
> of *spite*. The action may be sane, and the per-
> petrator may seem gratified, but we find it
> difficult to imagine his rational motivation. We
> refer to the commitment of a spiteful act as
> "all too human"—and then wonder what we
> meant (1975, p. 117).

Wilson, however, is at least equivocal about
the degree of consciousness people have of kin selection. He speaks, on one hand, of the human
mind's "intuitive calculus of blood ties"—a phrase
in some respects contradictory in itself—and on the
other hand, of people's keen awareness of such ties.
For example:

> The Hamilton models are beguiling in part be-
> cause of their transparency and heuristic value.
> The coefficient of relationship, *r*, translates
> easily into "blood," and the human mind, already

sophisticated in the intuitive calculus of blood ties and proportionate altruism, races to apply the concept of inclusive fitness to a revaluation of its own social impulses (ibid., pp. 119–20).

True spite is a commonplace in human societies, undoubtedly because human beings are keenly aware of their own blood lines and have the intelligence to plot intrigues (ibid., p. 119).

Now the notion of a secret wisdom of consanguinity, together with an unconscious system of algebra, however ridiculous, makes it extremely difficult to argue the point of kin selection anthropologically. The most careful demonstration of the lack of correspondance between degrees of genealogical relatedness and a given society's classifications of kinship can only hope to meet the reception that the anthropologist has been mystified by the same self-deceptions as the people concerned, that something else (biological) is really going on. There is really some hidden, disarticulated structure of genetic self-interest. We thus arrive at a point of argument where there is no appeal but to the facts. I have to insist from the outset—taking my stand on the whole of the ethnographic record—that the actual systems of kinship and concepts of heredity in human societies, though they never conform to biological coefficients of relationship, are true models of and for social action. These cultural determinations of "near" and "distant" kin make up the de facto form taken by shared interests and manifested in behaviors of altruism, antagonism, and the like. They represent the effective structures of sociability in the societies concerned, and accordingly bear directly on reproductive success. Indeed, as we shall see, the relation between the recognition of kinship and an appropriate mode of action is often reciprocal, such that the latter becomes testimony of the former and the people concerned, perhaps perfect strangers before the *act*, are ever after kinsmen for every intent and purpose but the genealogical. This is just what it means to construct a social world symbolically. And its possibility rests on just what kinship does mean in human societies, which is not genetic connection but quite generally, as in the English etymology of the term, people of the same "kind": a notion of social identity, permuted into a system of differential value (kinship categories) in terms of degrees and types of consubstantiality. Hence an act of "kindness" may be a performative demonstration of a relation of "kindred"—two words, as E. B. Tylor said, "whose common derivation expresses in the happiest way one of the most fundamental principles of social life."

My aim is to support the assertion that there is not a single system of marriage, postmarital residence, family organization, interpersonal kinship, or common descent in human societies that does not set up a different calculus of relationship and social action than is indicated by the principles of kin selection. I do so in two stages, passing from general ethnographic observations to the analysis of a critical case.

Consider first the structure of family groups and local kinship networks. Insofar as these are founded on any discriminating rule—normally it would be a rule of residence after marriage—they will comprise a determinate and biased proportion of any person's genealogical universe. From the point of view of a natural kinship, the bias would be twofold. It will consist of a selected sample of genetic kin, according to the residence rule, and it will position within the same group persons who are more distantly related to each other than they are to certain "kinsmen" living elsewhere. But insofar as these residential groups constitute domestic and cooperative associations engaged in intensive sharing or pooling of vital resources, mutual aid in production or joint production, perhaps holding property together and acting as units in marital exchange—all of which are ordinary practices of local kinship—then such biased congeries of relatives become the real units of reproductive success, thus differentiated from, and often explicitly in opposition to, their own nearer kin in other groups. All of this is Anthropology 101. Take a common rule such as patrilocal residence, with marriage outside the hamlet. By the rule, newly married couples live in the groom's father's household, thus generating an extended family of a man, his wife, his married sons with their spouses and children (family form found among approximately 34 percent of the world's societies, Murdock 1967).[1] By the same rule, the local hamlet—or it could be a territorial hunting band —is comprised of several such families whose heads are usually brothers or sons of brothers. A young man will thus find himself in collaboration with cousins of the first degree ($r = 1/8$) or greater degree ($r = 1/32$, $1/64$, etc.), uncles (FB, $r = 1/4$), quite possibly grand uncles (FFB, $r = 1/8$). If polygyny is practiced there will be even more distant kin within the family (e.g., F½BS, $r = 1/16$). Meanwhile, the sister ($r = 1/2$) of this same young man will go off to live with her husband upon marriage, raising her children ($r = 1/4$) in the latter's household; while his mother's sister ($r = 1/4$) has probably always resided elsewhere, as has his paternal aunt (r = 1/4) since her marriage. When he grows to maturity, our young man likewise loses his daughter (r = 1/2) and her children (r = 1/4) as also all other women born to his own extended family group, though he retains his son, his son's son and all males born to the group. Hence insofar as a man favors the "blood" kinsman of his group, he discriminates against those of equal or closer degree outside of it. Yet while all this stands in evident contradiction to the rationality of inclusive fitness, it will appear so only to the sociobiologist; because, as it concerns the people themselves, relatives who live together are "close" kinsmen while those who live apart are "distant" kinsmen. Regardless of genealogical degree, categories of kinship distance are pragmatically inflected by residence, inasmuch as membership in the same domestic group is a fundamental condition of *social* identity. This is a matter of common ethnographic report, such as, for example, Malinowski on the Mailu of New Guinea:

> Brothers living together, or a paternal uncle and his nephews living in the same house were, as far as my observation goes, on much closer terms with each other than relatives of similar degree living apart. This was evident whenever there was a question of borrowing things, of getting help, of accepting an obligation, or of assuming responsibilities for each other (1915, p. 532).

In the same vein, Paul Ottino reports that on Rangiroa Island in the Tuamotus—an ethnography to which we shall return: ". . . coresident relatives are, independently of their genealogical position, considered closer than non-residents" (1972, p. 168).

It may be objected that I have made the demonstration too easy by imposing a strict rule of marital residence. In fact the proof is easier, if in ethnographic annals it is rarer, where a person has the free choice of living with consanguineal kin of any kind. The To'ambaita of the Solomons reside in local property-holding groups of thirty to eighty people, each of which is focused on the symbolic testimony of their genealogical unity, a sacred grove sheltering the ancestral graves (Hogbin 1939). Because the group is small and near kin are prohibited from marrying, the greater part of the people, on average two-thirds, espouse members of other such "districts." Now in principle a person is entitled to take up residence and full membership in any group in which he has a consanguineal relative, male or female, and so by implication a common ancestry with others of that district. Since marriage is usually outside the district, most people have an immediate choice of affiliation with two groups, that of their mother or father. In fact, the option is often much wider, as by the same right one might reside in the place of any one of four grandparents, eight great-grandparents, and so forth. In practice the majority of men continue on after marriage in their father's place, which has the same implication of disparity between degrees of relationship and degrees of cooperation as strict patrilocal residence. But since residence is not strictly patrilocal and the groups are so small, the disparity is actually greater. Hogbin analyzes a representative district in which the nearest common ancestor of the whole stock is distant from living adults by nine generations. It follows that certain people of the group may have a coefficient of relationship as low as $(1/2)^{16} = 1/32,768$. Meanwhile, the same people have respectively mother's brothers ($r = 1/4$), mother's fathers ($r = 1/4$), mother's sisters ($r = 1/4$), maternal first cousins ($r = 1/8$), etc.—and/or paternal relatives of comparable degree, possibly also married sisters ($r = 1/2$) or brothers ($r = 1/2$)—living in and fully integrated with outside groups. Hogbin tells us that the districts stand in opposition to, and fear of sorcery from, one another. On the other hand, within the group there is not only a common right to resources but intense cooperation in production—and an intensity of sharing that is ten times the rate between groups (ibid., p. 28). The cultural organization of reproductive success, exactly as it is based on kinship properly so called, has nothing to do with an inclusive fitness calculated on biological connections.[2]

Since I have already introduced the cultural factor of descent—the To'ambaita districts being ancestrally based—let us turn more particularly to this modality of kinship structure. For exogamous unilineal descent groups, those organized prescriptively on the male (patrilineal) or female (matrilineal) line, analysis would show just the same kind of genealogical bias as attends patrilocal or matrilocal residence. Over time, the members of the descent unit comprise a smaller and smaller fraction of the ancestor's total number of genealogical descendants, diminishing by a factor of $1/2$ each generation. Assuming patrilineality, for example, and an equal number of male and female births, half the members in each generation are lost to the lineage, since the children of the women will be members of their husband's lineage. The actual rate of kin loss would depend on the total number of descent groups and the rule of intermarriage between them, as these factors will effect a certain recirculation of genetic descendants back into the original group. But in the abstract, by the third generation the group consists of only 1/4 the ancestor's genealogical kin, by the fifth generation, only 1/16, and so on. And whereas those of the fifth generation in the paternal line may have a coefficient of relationship of 1/256, each has relatives in other lineages— sister's children, mother's brothers, mother's sisters —whose r coefficient is as high as 1/4. Here again, insofar as the lineage is a cooperative and corporate group of joint estate, the factors determining reproductive success are organized independently of genealogical relationships. In the New Guinea Highlands, the line between one's own clan and other clans (or it may be between subclan and subclan) is a difference, as the Kuma put it, between a "together" relation and a "from-to" relation; which is to say, economically, between sharing and exchanging (Reay 1959, p. 93 et passim; cf. Brown and Brookfield 1959–60, p. 59, on the Chimbu). The ideology may extend to responsibilities of bride price, which is directly implicated in reproductive success:

> The criterion of clan membership [among the Daribi] is that of sharing wealth, as opposed to exchanging wealth. This is symbolized by the sharing or giving of meat; members of a clan "eat meat together" or "are given meat." A man cannot marry the sister or daughter of someone with whom he shares meat . . . marriage within the clan would necessitate an exchange of wealth among those who normally share wealth anyway and would be senseless. A clan is, therefore, necessarily exogamous, for marriage is a form of exchange, and clan members by definition share exchange rela-

tionships; that is, they contribute to each other's bride prices and share in the distribution of wealth received through exchange by one another (Wagner 1967, p. 145).

In dealing with descent groups, however, we cannot ignore the systems of marriage that interrelate them, for these introduce diverse valuations of kinds of kinsmen and corresponding permutations in the structure of sociabilities. The New Guinea Highlanders frequently have marriage rules of the "complex" type, negative rules that interdict a variety of kin unions and have the broad effect of "weak alliance": dispersing the marital relationships of any one lineage or clan rather than uniting it with a few others through the perpetual exchange of women (cf. Lévi-Strauss 1969). The result is a quasi-exclusive unity of the clan as against all others—hence, the famous aphorism of the Enga, "we fight the people we marry." In arrangements such as this, the women of the group, as it were, put an end to kinship: incorporated (with their children) in their husband's line, they are lost to their clan of birth, and relations traced through them suffer a change in quality (i.e., from "together" to "from-to"). In an analogous case, the Nuer of the Sudan would say, "A daughter, that is an unrelated person." Evans-Pritchard explains the implied difference in value between kinship through men and women:

. . . a daughter does not carry on the lineage of her father. She becomes one of her husband's people and her children belong to his lineage. Hence Nuer say: "*Nyal, mo ram me gwagh,*" 'A daughter, that is an unrelated person.' As the Roman lawyers put it, she is *finis familiae*, the terminus of the family. But a man's name must continue in his lineage, and Nuer consider it very wrong if a man who dies without male heirs is not married a wife by a kinsman who will raise up seed to him by her so that he will be remembered in his sons (1951, p. 109; the last allusion is to the famous "ghost marriage," to which we shall return).

But the concept of kinship through women is different where the passage of daughters between descent groups is the means of an enduring alliance (as in "elementary" systems with prescribed rules of kinship marriage). Here the woman is the *beginning* of kinship; Fijians say she is "holy blood" (*dra tabu*) because in her sons especially, she founds a new line as support for her group of birth. Her son (r [ego, SiSo] = 1/4) is accordingly a sacred person (*vasu*) relative to her brothers, i.e., their own mother's brothers, with special privileges of appropriating their goods without permission—a privilege a man would hardly allow his own son (r = 1/2) who in the same event is subject to a supernatural poisoning. Instead of fighting the people they marry, Fijians depend on them, and remarry these people with whom they coexist in perpetual peace. Thus the children of brothers and sisters ("cross cousins"), representing allied lines, must freely share their possessions, and certain of their children ("classificatory cross cousins") are again preferred marriage partners. There issues an interesting bias in the structure of a person's kin universe, rather the inverse of the unity of the lineage in the "complex" marriage systems. By the logic of the extended kinship terminology (which is technically "Dravidian" or "bifurcate merging"), a man should number as many "brothers" among his kinsmen as "cross cousins," and as many "fathers" as "mother's brothers." In fact, in one large Fijian village a sample of the relationships among a number of men produces the kind of results shown in table 1.

TABLE I

Relationship	Frequency
Brother–Brother	97
Cross cousin–Cross cousin	203
Father–Son	89
Mother's brother–Sister's son	127

Frequency of kin types among Naroi married men (after Sahlins 1962, p. 164).

The explanation of the unbalance in relations traced through women and men is this: brotherhood is, to say the least, an ambiguous relationship. As members of the same ranked lineage, brothers are paradigmatically rivals. Themselves ranked by birth order, their relations are marked by a sometimes onerous etiquette and privilege of economic command on the part of the elder whose exercise may well be resented by the younger. In contrast, brother and sister are not terminologically ranked; their interaction is characterized by mutual respect, and as we have seen, relationships traced through them are highly solidary. The reason, then, that there are many more such relationships than between brother and brother or father and son is that people choose the first when a choice is possible. Choice is possible when two people are connected in two different ways along nearly equal genealogical paths.

Furthermore, the same choice (in favor of cross cousinship) is mandatory when two people marry who had been distantly related as brother to sister or mother to son, event frequent enough. It is mandatory because the rule is that people marry their cross cousins. Hence the marriage is a performative act of cross cousinship, and relations between the immediate families concerned are transformed accordingly. The bride and groom and their respective siblings become cross cousins to each other, and the parents of each sibling set become (classificatory) mother's brother and father's sister to the other set. It is true that the second type of choice is partly consistent with kin selection, although the first is not. But both essentially depend on a valuation of the cross cousin ($r = 1/8$) over the brother ($r = 1/2$) that is in clear contrast to genetic amity, and only explicable by the cultural system of descent and alliance. Both choices, moreover, represent the distinctive quality of cultural order as a symbolic and creative force, not bound to express some natural kinship but to invent kinship in the first place as a social form. Such an invention is clearly seen in this: that whether kinship is traced through two brothers or a brother and sister constitutes a fundamental social difference, though it makes no genetic difference.

In the East African Sudan, dead men marry, and barren women are fathers. For the Nuer, a woman who does not bear children counts as a man. If she can amass cattle through bride-price dues and the trade of magic, she espouses one or more other women in regular marital rites. Her wives are impregnated by a kinsman, friend, neighbor, sometimes by a member of a subordinate tribe (Dinka). But the biological father is merely the *genitor* of her children; the woman herself is the true or legal father (*pater*), as she is the legal husband of their mothers. She controls the marriage of her daughters ($r = x$ or 0), and she and her siblings receive the bride-price cattle due the father's side. She is evidently addressed as "father" by her children. And, "she administers her home and herd as a man would do, being treated by her wives and children with the deference they would show to a male husband and father" (Evans-Pritchard 1951, p. 109). As for ghost marriage (see p. 33), it establishes a legal household consisting of the ghost, in whose name the marriage ceremonies are performed, together with his wives, children, and the genitor of the children, usually a brother or close lineage mate of the deceased. One might argue that the practice in itself does not violate kin selection since it merely involves the social substitution of (purportedly) genetic kin. Yet it is witness to a concept of human continuity that has the opposite sense of an egotistical reproductive success. In kin selection a man sacrifices himself purposefully for the reproductive success of his brothers. In ghost marriage, a man devotes his seed to the perpetuation of a brother who may well have died accidentally, or simply proven incapable of siring a male heir, that is, for a man who in an absolute or culturally relative sense has been selected against. The point of the example, however, is not that. The points is that *for human beings, survival is not figured in terms of life and death or as the number of genes one transmits to succeeding generations.* Humans do not perpetuate themselves as physical but as social beings. Death is not the end of a man, nor even of his reproductive ability. Men alone are immortal. They live on as *names* and in the *memory* of those they left behind, as well as in the form of spirits who may enjoy every satisfaction known to the living (or even more so). For their existence continues to be manifest and reckoned in the social arrangements of their survivors. And in many human societies, the prospects of such an existence may motivate a man during his lifetime to acts that are the reverse of all egotism. It is well known that it is easier for a camel to pass through the eye of a needle than for a rich man to enter the kingdom of heaven.

In the Trobriand Islands, a matrilineal society, the cultural system of reproduction and perpetuation is the opposite of that of the patrilineal Nuer. A man, who is a member of an alien group relative to his children (they belong to their mother's and mother's brother's subclan) contributes absolutely nothing of his physical substance to his offspring. As reported by Malinowski, the act of copulation itself is not considered the cause of birth; there is no concept of a genitor at all. A child receives his internal and essential self, his soul, through the impregnation of the mother by a spirit (*baloma*) of her matrilineal subclan floating over the waters from the land of souls. The sense of this fairy tale with which the Trobrianders seem to deceive themselves is that the child belongs wholly to—and so is the incarnation of—the matrilineal group. The father contributes only to the appearance of the child and shapes the child by the loving care he provides it in infancy, just as the father's side (father's sisters) decorate a man with ornaments during critical rituals of his life. By reason of these understandings of maternal nature and paternal nurture, Trobrianders insist that children resemble their fathers since the latter have molded them; they are shocked by the suggestion that children may resemble their

mothers or her kinsmen, who have nonetheless provided their inherited substance! Upon maturity,
young men normally leave the household of their
father for the village of their mother's brother,
where they have full legal status and land rights.
Sometimes, out of enduring sentiment and the desire to have his sons about him, acting as buffers
to the contentions of his sister's sons, a chief especially may retain his sons and secure them use-rights
in his own subclan's lands; but the position of such
sons in their father's place is never secure unless
they marry their father's sister's daughter, which
makes their own children again full members of
the local (matrilineal) subclan. On the other hand,
a father is in certain pragmatic contexts a "stranger" or an "outsider" relative to his own children,
not a true blood (in this case, soul) relative. "The
father, in all discussions about relationship, was
pointedly described to me as *tomakava*, a 'stranger,'
or, even more correctly, an 'outsider.' This expression
would frequently be used by natives in conversa-
tion, when they were arguing some point of inheritance or trying to justify some line of conduct, or
again when the position of the father was to be
belittled in some quarrel" (Malinowski 1929, p. 5).
Indeed, since the determination of "fatherhood"
in the first place is not sexual, "fathers" will in
perfect equanimity raise children who cannot be
genetically their own. The father of the child is once
again, and quite sufficiently, the husband of the
mother:

> A man whose wife has conceived during his
> absence will cheerfully accept the fact and the
> child, and he will see no reason for suspecting
> her of adultery. One of my informants told me

that after over a year's absence he returned to find a newly born child at home. He volunteered this statement as an illustration and final proof of the truth that sexual intercouse has nothing to do with conception. . . .

There is another instance of a native of the small island of Kitava, who, after two years' absence, was quite pleased to find a few months' old baby at home, and could not in the slightest degree understand the indiscreet taunts and allusions of some white men with reference to his wife's virtue (ibid., p. 193).[3]

One need not belabor the evident point about genetic self-interest. More important is the cultural concept that underlies all such apparent violations of natural selection and motivates a structure of human kinship that alone can account for the empirical form of an individual's social interest. Here it is, as in many other descent systems, that biological inheritance is not an individual function at all; for a child does not receive his genetic makeup from either of his parents, let alone by some diploid process discovered by twentieth-century biologists. The child is the incarnation of the genetic pool, if it may be so called, of his matrilineal subclan. True, he is the reincarnation of some dead member of this subclan, but the spirits that come from the land of souls to impregnate a woman are not considered to have any individuality. They are not in this respect specific ancestors; they are merely specific manifestations of the collective subclan substance. It follows that the matrilineal descent group is a single entity in organic heritage. Its members have a coefficient of relationship of 1, they are of one flesh and one blood, even as their coefficient of relationship with their fathers equals 0 (cf. ibid., p. 200). To put it another way, the subclan itself is the unit of reproduction in the Trobriand Islands. With regard to this concept of social reproduction, human mating affords little interest, no knowledge, and no project of individual behavior.

Before passing to the detailed analysis of a specific case, it may be well to recapitulate a few of the empirical inconveniences posed to the theory of kin selection by the ethnography already on hand. All such inconveniences follow from the more general observation that the structure of social interest is not constituted by individual genetic interests. The ethnographic facts are that the members of the kinship groups which organize human reproduction are more closely related genealogically to persons outside the group than to certain others within. As membership in kin associations may be secured performatively, and in any case it is the group which reproduces itself as a social unit, reproductive benefits are often accorded to persons unrelated genetically—who may easily be one's own children (in the cultural order). At the same time, the discontinuities between the ethnographic topology of benefit relations and the natural structure of consanguinity generates irrationalities in the cost/benefit program alleged to control social behavior. Since genetic distance increases geometrically, the presence of, say, second cousins ($r = 1/32$) within the category of cooperating kin will require enormous costs in altruism in order to derive any personal fitness gains, even as the relative efficacy of helping nearer kin, perhaps brothers or sisters, is impeded or precluded by their distribution in outside groups of distinct interest. If, however, one fails to meet the algebraic requirements of fitness in regard to the people with whom one shares a social interest—for second cousins, a return on altruism more than thirty-two times the cost to oneself—then the services provided to them select against one's own reproductive success. If, moreover, the beneficial relations within a category of cooperating kin are more or less reciprocal, which is everywhere the case though the people concerned be relatively distant genealogically, then no *differential* individual advantage accrues to any given ego (see pp. 83–88, on "reciprocal altruism"). Of course the cooperating group may be thus favored reproductively over other groups, but that is exactly the cultural point, and in direct contrast to a genetics of competitive self-interest. Finally, the violation of individual genetic rationality is compounded by the political as well as economic counterposition of descent or kindred segments, so that in favoring the home group, though it include distant kin and strangers, one is discriminating against persons of equal or closer genealogical degree in other groups.

Polynesia offers us privileged sites for testing the theory of kin selection. It is something like Durkheim's one well-chosen experiment that can prove (or disprove) a scientific law. The case is privileged because to all appearances the Polynesian societies afford structural conditions that are favorable to the operation of kin selection. In these island societies, descent may be bilaterally reckoned ("cognatic"), rather than the kind of patriliny or matriliny that a priori renders the thesis of kin selection vulnerable; analogously, residence is often optional, with either the mother's kin or the father's, and the people are notoriously mobile. They are also famous for the value they attach to genealogies, which in some instances range back forty generations and more. Finally, their own theory of heredity conforms to that of scientific biology, at least to the extent that children are equally of the "blood" of the mother and the father. In traditional Tahitian ceremonies of marriage and birth, this theory is iconically dramatized by combining blood taken from the relatives of the bride and groom respectively and applying it in one way or another to the ritual principals (the man and wife or their infant). Outside of the Western society, I can think of no place besides Polynesia where the idea that social action is fundamentally motivated by individual self-interest would have a better chance of being developed.[4]

Accordingly, the Polynesian societies merit a somewhat extended anthropological treatment, especially those of central and eastern Polynesia where bilaterality is most marked. I concentrate on the atoll of Rangiroa in the Tuamotus, subject of a recent monograph by Paul Ottino (1972) with some reference as well to Tahiti and Hawaii. According to Ottino, the structure of Rangiroan society rests on the unity of two groups, ordered at different levels of hierarchy or inclusiveness. There is first the sibling unit of brothers and sisters. These with their descendants over two generations make up the core of the elementary residential and proprietary groups, domiciled in a single domestic compound and holding a unified claim to land. A sibling set is known as 'ôpû ho'e, "one belly," that is, of the same womb, and the term is accordingly applied to the entire elementary kin group constituted by this key relation. Beyond the 'ôpû ho'e is the âti, a bilateral descent group composed of several such brother-sister units descended from a common ancestor and comprising a larger, more inclusive property group. I will take up these groups in order, beginning with the calculus of kin relationships and solidarities at the elementary level of the brother-sister-based corporations.

In discussing Rangiroa, one uses such phrases as the "unity of the group" or the "unity of siblings" advisedly, not just out of deference to Radcliffe-Brown's famous formulas of kinship order.[5] The people say that any group of brothers and sisters are "the same" or "identical" (*ho'e â*). They are "one blood" (*toto ho'e*), as they share the blood of their mother and father. Yet if Rangiroans thus recognize descent from both parents, they do not have a genetic theory of meiosis, so for them the coefficient of relationships between siblings is 1 rather than the 1/2 of Western biology. (The social and hereditary identity of the brother-sister set is a general principle in Polynesia, and beyond that among Malayo-Polynesian speakers as far as Indonesia and Taiwan. There is reason to believe that it is also the true folk concept of Western societies.) All further calculations of kinship distance in Rangiroa presuppose the inherent unity of siblings. These calculations may be a little difficult for us to understand. Customarily having in mind the image of kinship as a genealogically ordered space, Westerners (notably including anthropologists) are prone to think of kinship distance as extending along two dimensions, the vertical and horizontal planes of the genealogical chart, corresponding to degrees of lineality and degrees of collaterality. But since by Rangiroan conceptions, siblings are one, for them collaterality may be ignored, or rather it is subsumed by lineality. In Rangiroan reckoning, the sole measure of distance among kinsmen descended from the same ancestor is generational. Each generation counts as one degree of remove, and collateral relatives are as distant as the number of generational steps required to reach the common ancestor. This is entirely consistent with their understanding of "descent," which is perhaps more properly spoken of as "ascent." The ancestor is the "root" (e.g., Fijian, *vu*) or "source" (e.g., Hawaiian, *kumu*) of the genealogical tree from which his descendants have grown and branched out. So Tahitians say, *naafea raaua i au?* "how are they-two linked?": *na ni? a e tupuna i raro rooa*, "through an ancestor far below" (Hooper 1970a, p. 314). Hence for the Rangiroans, if siblings are "one blood," first cousins are "two bloods," second cousins "three bloods," and so on to "five bloods" (fourth cousins) which is an important pragmatic limit to "kinship" (*feti'i*), as boundary to the prohibition on intermarriage. This means that for Polynesians kinship distance is figured arithmetically, beginning from a cultural determination of siblings as "one"; whereas, for biologists it progresses geometrically, according to their concepts of meiosis. For biologists, the coefficient of relationships among siblings, first cousins and second cousins passes from 1/2, to 1/8, to 1/32, respectively, as compared to the Rangiroan 1, 2, 3. The latter would thus experience some difficulty figuring the egotistic algebra of kin selection posed as a general social logic by the former. Moreover, as we shall see momentarily, the ordering of "bloods" is often reversed in social practice, as people of "four bloods" or "five bloods" may be considered closer kinsmen than those of "two" or "three"; while on the basis of the pragmatic equivalence of coresidence and siblingship, distinctions of "blood" are subordinated to the unity of "one belly" (*'ôpû ho'e*).

(In passing it needs to be remarked that the epistemological problems presented by a lack of linguistic support for calculating r, coefficients of relationship, amount to a serious defect in the theory of kin selection. Fractions are of very rare occurrence in the world's languages, appearing in Indo-European and in the archaic civilizations of the Near and Far East, but they are generally lacking among the so-called primitive peoples. Hunters and gatherers generally do not have counting systems beyond *one*, *two*, and *three*. I refrain from comment on the even greater problem of how animals are supposed to figure out how that r [ego, first cousins] = 1/8. The failure of sociobiologists to address this problem introduces a considerable mysticism in their theory. Or at least, without an explanation of the exact algebraic mechanics, the theory becomes vulnerable to what Wilson describes [after Northrup] as "the Fallacy of Affirming the Consequent." This fallacy, Wilson writes, "takes the form of constructing a particular model from a set of postulates, obtaining a result, noting that approximately the predicted result does exist in nature, and concluding thereby that the postulates are true. The difficulty is that a second set of postulates, inspiring a different model, can often lead to the same result. It is even possible to start with the same conditions, construct wholly different models from them, and still arrive at the same result" [1975, p. 29]. Of course, this particular criticism is not really germane to the present discussion since for humans the theory of kin selection does not arrive at the predicted empirical results in the first place.[6])

In Rangiroa, the reckoning of relationships up to "three bloods" (second cousins) is of special social significance because the group of descendants from a common stock of brothers and sisters at the grandparental generation constitutes the nucleus of the elementary domestic and proprietary units. These basic social segments, the *'ôpû ho'e* ("one belly") are thus in principle bilateral or cognatic groups. However, it must be considered that in cognatic systems, there is always a pragmatic factoring of genealogical distance by other considerations, notably common residence, if the groups formed on the basis of descent are actually to function as definite domestic and property units. This is because each member of the group is potentially a member of as many such groups as he has ancestors. As in the example of the To'ambaita (*supra*), a given person has an equally legitimate claim to membership in the distinct sibling groups of his four grandparents or his eight great-grandparents. Seen another way, if a person's father has one brother and one sister, then that ego and his first cousins on the paternal side alone potentially belong to six different cognatic groups—they descend from six different sibling sets on the grandparental generation—only two of which overlap (being the *'ôpû ho'e* of ego's FF and FM). Even a single set of brothers and sisters, although they are "the same," could easily and legitimately be divided between their mother's and father's respective ancestral compounds, for recall that residence is optional and may be frequently changed. The principle of common bilateral descent results in overlapping membership categories, hence it must be "restricted" by some other principle if it is to be the criterion of independent householding and property groups. The normal mode of restriction is coresidence. In the event, the unity of the sibling group and their descendants is selectively factored by the choice of residence; or rather, such unity is pragmatically substantialized by coresidence, so that for culturally (and biologically) strategic contexts as

solidarity, mutual aid, coproduction and coproprie-
torship, the measure of kinship distance depends on
which people are actually living together. We have
already encountered Ottino's general observation to
this effect: "coresident relatives are, independently
of their genealogical position, considered closer than
non-residents" (1972, p. 168).

Furthermore, since the close relationship of co-
residents is realized in appropriate kinship terms
and behaviors, the effect over time is to subordinate
the structure of distance implied by the genealogy
to the structure of residential sociability embodied
in the terms. Kinship usages no longer follow genealogical relations, as "a good number" of the latter
"are simply ignored" (ibid., p. 188). If "not exact"
from the point of view of consanguinity, the code of
kinship terms, together with the appropriate code of
morality, prevails nonetheless because the people
"do not know the exact genealogical relations and
care little to know them" (ibid., p. 189). What happens is that the genealogies are reinvented to make
them logically consistent with the terms (ibid., pp.
188–89, et passim). Genealogy is deduced from kinship, rather than kinship from genealogy.

Specifically, the Rangiroa have a pragmatic
code of who is "one belly" or even "one blood,"
and who acts accordingly toward whom, which depends on the reciprocal definition of kinship by residence and residence by kinship. Their formula is:
"one *'ôpû* (belly); one *aua fare* (walled-domestic
compound), one *fare tupuna* (ancestral house)." The
satisfaction of any one of these criteria is ipso facto
an entitlement to the others. People who live in the
same domestic compound are "one belly"; they have
satisfied the cultural conditions of consanguinity (for
all practical purposes). Half siblings who are raised

together in the same household are considered "one blood," albeit this contradicts the Rangiroan theory of "bloods" not less than our own. Again adopted children are "one belly" with the natural children of the household and with each other, though they may be "strangers" without genealogical connection to some or all of their siblings. (Since adoption is, like marriage, a mode of alliance between groups, such children retain "blood" in their natal families as well, the dual descent being effaced only over genealogical time. But in the effective kinship context of residence, adoptive children are not only "one belly," they consider themselves "the same" [ho'e â] as their brothers and sisters of the house [pp. 192–93], an expression taken as equivalent to "one blood" [pp. 207–8], which equivalence in turn is the means of eventual assimilation of genealogical to residential kinship.) And all children of the house, whether "natural," stepchildren or adopted, have the same rights of inheritance and paternal care, as well as complete solidarity as siblings with each other. Residence and not biology thus defines the de facto kinship, for, after all, as one Rangiroa man put it to Ottino, "au hasard des coucheries tu peux être feti'i [relative] avec n'importe qui ('by the chances of sleeping around you could be the kinsman of no matter whom')" (ibid.).

A word on adoption. Not only Rangiroa, but Polynesia generally is famous for adoption practices that violate the moral logic of kin selection with regard to parental care, concern for one's own offspring as against those of genetic competitors, etc. Indeed, in traditional Tahiti it was proper practice to adopt the child or nearest kinsman of an enemy one had slain in war (Oliver 1974, vol. 2, p. 703). There is, moreover, a high probability that the adopting parent in this case will have slain one or more of his own (natural) children at birth. For infanticide in Tahiti, as in Hawaii, reached extraordinary proportions. The considered judgment of the most qualified modern student of Tahitian society is that, "there was hardly a 'married' woman alive who had not lost at least one offspring in this manner" (ibid., vol. 1, p. 425). On the other hand, the women who had thus debarrassed themselves of children at one time would at another welcome into their households the children of others—on an equal practical footing with their own. Despite lack of official or religious encouragement, adoption in modern Tahiti is still 25 percent of all children born; in the rural community of Maupiti, 38 percent of the households include adopted children (Hooper 1970b). The Hawaiian figures are of the same order (Howard 1970; Ellis 1969 [1842]).

The unusually high infanticide needs special explanation. The explanation would not be without interest to certain other predictions from the theory of kin selection to the effect that all of a given parent's children, since they have an equal proportion of his or her genes $(1/2)$, should be given equal care (resources permitting). If the success of any one child is favored over the others, it would not be in the interest of the parent's inclusive fitness, a clear violation of the formula $k > 1/\bar{r}$. In fact, one of the reasons for Tahitian and Hawaiian infanticide, especially among chiefs and other prominent people, appears as an indirect result of the social and reproductive advantages accorded to one child at the expense of his siblings. In Tahiti, the firstborn son was ritually installed as his father's successor at birth, and rendered many other privileges—the Hawaiians analogously had a specific category of "fa-

vored child" on whom attention was extravagantly
lavished—which had the effect of forestalling competition from younger brothers. In the same interest,
disenfranchised sons might have a substantially
smaller chance of marrying and raising up contend-
ing lineages. There was no bar, however, to their
sexual activity, so long as it did not have living issue.
In Tahiti, many of the cadet sons evidently joined
the famous class of entertainers (*ariori*), a group of
thousands, by some estimates one-fifth of the population, who were notorious at once for their sexual
license and the rule that any who bore living children
were excluded from active membership. Infanticide,
then, was in part a resolution of the problem of the
younger brother. In another part, infanticide re-
solved the equally political problem that would be
posed by the presence of illegitimate children of high
descent among lower orders of the population—occasioned again by the sexual liberties enjoyed by
people of rank. In Tahiti particularly, the offspring
of parents of different rank were usually killed.
(Thus it need not be supposed that the favoring of
one child at the expense of his siblings was an
adaptive response to scarcity—for which there is no
good evidence in any case—since the practice increases in proportion to social rank, thus in proportion to prior and preemptive rights to resources.)
The analogue in Hawaii was a general condition in
all ranks of a prolonged adolescence, perhaps to the
age of twenty or twenty-five, which may be attributed to certain land arrangements by which a man
would have to delay settling down until he could
replace a deceased householder of the senior generation on his own or his wife's family lands. In the
interval, men and women were highly mobile and
without sexual frustration, but any children born of

their youthful liaisons were liable to infanticide (Malo 1839). Yet the households that these same people eventually founded were very likely to include adopted children sired by others.

In the light of such customs, or the willingness of Trobriand "fathers" to raise children born to their wives during their own absence of years, the following statement of the sociobiologist Alexander has a special theoretical interest:

> Darwin, after all, had noted (1859, p. 201) that "If it could be proved that any part of the structure of any one species had been formed for the exclusive good of another species, it would annihilate my theory, for such could not have been produced by natural selection." . . . Neither Darwin or any of his successors thought to emphasize the obvious conclusion that follows from his 1859 challenge, and is even more appropriate and startling. To find an adaptation in an individual that evolved because its sole or net effect is to assist a reproductive competitor within the same species, would also annihilate Darwin's entire theory (Alexander 1975, pp. 81–82).

I leave it to biologists to draw their own conclusions. As for the keen awareness that E. O. Wilson supposes people to have of their own blood ties, that "intuitive calculus of blood ties" on which their sociability is algebraically predicated, consider this statement of a modern Hawaiian woman on her relation to her adopted brother's child Kealoha:

> Kealoha is my brother's child. Of course my brother isn't really my brother as both he and I

are *hanai* [adoptive] children of my father. I guess my father isn't really my father, is he? I know who my real mother is, but I didn't like her and I never see her. My *hanai* brother is half-Hawaiian and I am pure Hawaiian. We aren't really any blood relations I guess, but I always think of him as my brother and I always think of my [adoptive] father as my father. I think maybe Papa [her adoptive father] is my grandfather's brother; I'm not sure as we never asked such things. So I don't know what relation Kealoha really is, though I call her my child (Howard 1970, p. 43).

Returning to Rangiroa, the larger descent groups (*âti*) are composed on the same kinship principles as their householding constituents (*'ôpû ho'e*). One may think of the *âti* as a kind of "one belly" of higher order, for its members share hereditary substance and are again at this level a genealogical unity. Consequently the *âti* are said by the Rangiroans to be distinguished by certain physiognomic traits and psychological dispositions:

The Polynesian ideas relative to heredity are such that all members of the same *âti* are reputed to share certain common physical and psychological traits . . . which are "positively" manifest by particular aptitudes or qualities or "negatively" by imperfections, eccentricities or faults, which may mercilessly be brought up and ridiculed in *to'a*, sorts of defamatory sobriquets by which the people who are not members of the *âti* make fun of its members (Ottino 1972, pp. 240–41).

As a hereditary unit, the *âti* enters into complex relationships with the unity of the sibling group to practically determine the degree of kinship between any two persons. The relation is frequently complex because of the bilateral (cognatic) character of solidarity and group membership operating simultaneously at different social levels, such that a person may have genealogically closer kin in different *âti* than he has in his own. In the vectorial determination of kinship degree that ensues, genealogical connection often proves to have less force than the factor of coresidence and group affiliation. Kinship distance is also affected by religious differences and various personal oppositions, but I will leave these aside in commenting on Ottino's excellent illustration of the inflection of relationships by *âti* membership (fig. 1).

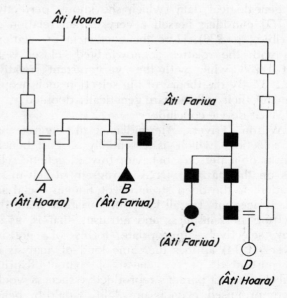

Fig. 1. Genealogical relations and kinship distance, Rangiroa (adapted from Ottino 1972, p. 236).

Informant *B*, Ottino tells us, was quite equivocal about the "closeness" of his kinship to *A*, despite the fact that they are first cousins. On the one hand, he said that *A* was "close"; but then he qualified this in various ways. *B*, however, was clear about his relationship to *C*: she was a "close relative" of his. The problem with the relation *A–B* is that although they are only "two bloods" removed they belong to different households (*'ôpû ho'e*) and different *âti*, whereas *C* is the same *âti* as *B*. So *B* feels unambiguously closer to *C* than to *A*, despite the genealogical disparity this involves: $r(B,A) = 1/8$, while $r(B,C) = 1/16$. Likewise, informant *D* held that *A* was a close relative by common *âti*. But "with equal conviction and in flagrant contradiction with the genealogical data (which she knows perfectly) she [*D*] considers herself a very distant relation of *C*" (ibid., p. 236). Here the coefficient of relationship with the relative acknowledged "close" is at least 1/258, while with the "very distant" relative it is 1/32. By the theory of kin selection such people —and/or their culture—are genetically doomed.[7]

What do we conclude?

Wilson, Trivers, Alexander et al. suggest that kin selection, which is essentially a cost/benefit analysis of a person's behavior toward genetic relatives on the basis of DNA's program of self-maximization, is the deep structure of human social action. It accounts for all kinds of variation along the spectrum of selfishness and altruism, that is, as so many selectively appropriate forms of egotism. Trivers (1974) applies the same kind of analysis to the purported pervasiveness of parent-offspring conflict—since a parent's reproductive success would be compromised, even as any child's would be benefited, by a degree of "parental investment" (i.e., child care) that goes beyond the 1/2 genetic interest a parent holds in any one child and the equal interest he or she holds in every other child. Trivers is wont to take as evidence of the generality of parent-child conflict in "humans" the folk experience that Western social psychologists discover in controlled experiments. For him it is always possible to consider the behavior of American adolescent girls or London nursery tots as testimony of universal human propensities (e.g., 1971; 1972). The characteristic adoption by sociobiologists of an economic discourse suggests the same kind of ethnocentric problem. Discussing kin selection, they have been all too prepared to allege as qualities of humanity as a whole the attributes of a society that does go so far as to consider its own children as "assets" (cf. Chicago School of Economics). But as the Maori proverbially say, "The troubles of other lands are their own." The concept of kin selection or, for that matter, of natural selection, developed by sociobiology is pecularily appropriate to a system of production that encompasses also human labor in the status of a commodity. Here indeed men must sell the use of themselves to others whose interest lies in an increasing reproduction of their own (capital) stock: a system, thus, in which the fundamental social relations are those of exchange with an eye singular to the net transfer of reproductive powers. Perhaps it was Marx who first revealed the historical specificity of the ideology of kin selection:

> The apparent stupidity of merging all the manifold relationships of people in the *one* relation of usefulness, this apparently metaphysical abstraction arises from the fact that, in modern bourgeois society, all relations are subordinated

in practice to the one abstract monetary-com-
mercial relation. This theory came to the fore
with Hobbes and Locke. . . . In Holbach, all
the activity of individuals in their mutual intercourse, e.g., speech, love, etc., is depicted as a
relation of utility and utilisation. Hence the
actual relations that are presupposed here are
speech, love, the definite manifestations of
definite qualities of individuals. Now these
relations are supposed not to have the meaning
peculiar to them but to be the expression and
manifestation of some third relation introduced
in their place, the relation of *utility or utilisation*. [≡ Terror]. . . .

All this is actually the case with the bourgeois. For him only *one* relation is valid on its
own account—the relation of exploitation; all
other relations have validity for him only insofar as he can include them under this one relation, and even where he encounters relations
which cannot be directly subordinated to the
relation of exploitation, he does at least subordinate them to it in his imagination. . . .
Incidentally, one sees at a glance that the category of "utilisation" is first of all abstracted
from the actual relations of intercourse which
I have with other people (but by no means from
reflection and mere will) and then these relations
are made out to be the reality of the category
that has been abstracted from them themselves,
a wholly metaphysical method of procedure
(Marx and Engels 1965, pp. 460–61).

Our discussion of the kinship-based societies,
which constitute the historic converse of appropria-
tive and possessive individualism, and, so far as

representative status in history is concerned, the normal human condition, supports the following judgments on the theory of kin selection.

First, no system of human kinship relations is organized in accord with the genetic coefficients of relationship as known to sociobiologists. Each consists from this point of view of arbitrary rules of marriage, residence, and descent, from which are generated distinctive arrangements of kinship groups and statuses, and determinations of kinship distance that violate the natural specifications of genealogy. Each kinship order has accordingly its own theory of heredity or shared substance, which is never the genetic theory of modern biology, and a corresponding pattern of sociability. Such human *conceptions* of kinship may be so far from biology as to exclude all but a small fraction of a person's genealogical connections from the category of "close kin"; while, at the same time, including in that category, as sharing common blood very distantly related people or even complete strangers. Among those strangers (genetically) may be one's own children (culturally).

Second, as the culturally constituted kinship relations govern the real processes of cooperation in production, property, mutual aid, and marital exchange, the human systems ordering reproductive success have an entirely different calculus than that predicted by kin selection and, *sequitur est*, by an egotistically conceived natural selection. Indeed, the relation between pragmatic cooperation and kinship definition is often reciprocal. If close kinsmen live together, then those who live together are close kin. If kinsmen make gifts of food, then gifts of food make kinsmen—the two are symbolically interconvertible forms of the transfer of substance. For as kinship is a code of conduct and not merely of reference, let alone genealogical reference, conduct becomes a code of kinship. We can be sure, then, that the categories of kinship are eminently practical, precisely in the measure that they are freely conceptual—and so become the very language of social experience.[8]

Yet as Durkheim taught, there is no social experience for men apart from its conceptualization, and in the matter at hand it follows that giving birth is just as much a pretext of kinship as giving gifts. The first is equally subject to a social interpretation of relationships, and no more beholden than the second to genetic axioms. A third conclusion, then, is that kinship is a unique characteristic of human societies, distinguishable precisely by its freedom from natural relationships. When sociobiologists use the term "kinship," and mean by that "blood" connections, they imagine they are invoking the common tongue, and the common experience, of men and animals, or at least of men as animals. For them, this pre-Babelian concept refers to nothing else than facts of life: a connected series of procreative acts, upon which natural selection must operate. Yet in cultural practice it is birth that serves as the metaphor of kinship, not kinship as the expression of birth. Birth itself is nothing apart from the kinship system which defines it. But as an event within this cultural order, birth becomes the functional index of certain values of childhood and parentage, values which are never the only ones conceivable yet which integrate the persons concerned, within and beyond the family, in ways independent of their degrees of genetic connection. The relationships that may be traced on genealogical lines, such as matrilineal or patrilineal descent,

respond to considerations of social identity and opposition external to the biological nexus as such;
they are relationships imposed upon it, that organize
it in the interest of a relative social scheme—and
thereby distort it. This does not mean people will
not trace their genealogies more or less widely and
bilaterally. On the contrary, they will do so precisely because different kinds of consanguineal links
are used to operate such distinctions as in-group
and out-group and to stipulate the relations between them. So bilateral reckoning, for example,
can be expected to become important just in the
measure that patrilineal or matrilineal descent
introduces a bias of kinship solidarity since it is the
difference of kinship through males or females—
itself irrelevant to genetic distance—that makes all
the difference in social behavior. Genealogy thus
serves to situate individuals in relation to one another, but according to qualitative values of solidarity that could never be discovered in the genetic
connections as such.

Hence we say that the determination of kinship
through acts of birth is just as arbitrary and creative as its establishment through acts of exchange or
residence. Furthermore, as in the case of "aggression" and other human dispositions, the various
emotions that may be mobilized around birth,
though they be potentialities of biological evolution
itself, are given a social effect only by the meanings
(i.e., the kinship) culturally assigned to the event.
Unique in this capacity of creative interpretation,
humans alone formulate systems of kinship properly so-
called; even as genealogy, being the product of this
same capacity, operates in human society as the
ideology of kinship, not its source. Because kinship
categories give arbitrary values to genealogical re-

lationships, sociobiologists have been forced to suppose that the categories are cultural mystifications of truer biological practices. It would be more accurate to say that insofar as kinship employs a code of births, it is a genealogical mystification of truly cultural practices. Paradoxically, then, whenever we see people ordering their social life on the premises of genealogy, it is good evidence that they are violating the dictates of genetics.

Fourth, it follows that human beings do not merely reproduce as physical or biological beings but as social beings: not in their capacities as self-mediating expressions of an entrepreneurial DNA but in their capacities as members of families and lineages, and in their statuses as cross cousins and chiefs. It follows too that what is reproduced in human cultural orders is not human beings *qua* human beings *but the system of social groups, categories, and relations in which they live*. The entities of social reproduction are precisely these culturally formulated groups and relations. Individuals of the same group may then figure as particulate expressions of the same inherent substance: they have a coefficient of relationship of 1, whatever their genealogical distance. Conversely, their own persistence is not figured individually or as the mortality chances of their own genetic stock. They have an eternal existence as names as well as a spiritual destiny as ancestors or great men, for which the only guarantee may be a moral existence during life far removed from the selfish demands of an inclusive fitness. In these senses it can be understood that human reproduction is engaged as the means for the persistence of cooperative social orders, not the social order the means by which individuals facilitate their own reproduction.

The final, most fundamental conclusion must be that culture is the indispensable condition of this system of human organization and reproduction, with all its surprises for the biogenetic theory of social behavior. Human society is cultural, unique in virtue of its construction by symbolic means. E. O. Wilson says, "the highest form of tradition, by whatever criterion we choose to judge it, is of course human culture. But culture, aside from its involvement with language, which is truly unique, differs from animal tradition only in degree" (1975, p. 168). Literally, the statement is correct. If we were to disregard language, culture would differ from animal tradition only in degree. But precisely because of this "involvement with language"—a phrase hardly befitting serious scientific discourse —cultural social life differs from the animal in kind. It is not just the expression of an animal of another kind. The reason why human social behavior is not organized by the individual maximization of genetic interest is that human beings are not socially defined by their organic qualities but in terms of symbolic attributes; and a symbol is precisely a meaningful value—such as "close kinship" or "shared blood"—which cannot be determined by the physical properties of that to which it refers.

Wilson pays lip service (if one may so put it) to this famous "arbitrary character of the sign." But for him the theoretical importance of human speech lies in its *function of communication* rather than its *structure of signification*, so it is primarily understood to *convey information* rather than to *generate meaning* (cf. Eco 1976). As communication, language is not distinguishable from the class of animal signaling, it only adds (quantitatively) to the capacity to signal. What is signaled is information

—which may be measured, as in classic theory, by the practical alteration in the behavior of the recipient from some otherwise probable course of action (negative entropy; cf. Wilson 1975, p. 10). This functional view of language, which incidentally is exactly Malinowski's, is particularly appropriate to a biological standpoint, for by it human speech is automatically subsumed in the adaptive action of responding to the natural or given world. What is lost by it is the creative action of constructing a human world: that is, by the sedimentation of meaningful values on "objective" differences according to local schemes of significance. So far as its concept or meaning is concerned, a word is not simply referrable to external stimuli but first of all to its place in the system of language and culture, in brief to its *own* environment of related words. By its contrast with these is constructed its own valuation of the object, and the totality of such valuations is a cultural constitution of "reality."

What is here at stake is the understanding that each human group orders the objectivity of its experience, including the biological "fact" of relatedness, and so makes of human perception and social organization a historic conception. Human communication is not a simple stimulus-response syndrome, bound thus to represent the material exigencies of survival. For the objectivity of objects is itself a cultural determination, generated by the assignment of a symbolic significance to certain "real" differences even as others are ignored. On the basis of this segmentation or *découpage*, the "real" is systematically constituted, that is, in a given cultural mode. Cassirer explains:

An "objective" representation—it is this which I wish to explain—is not the point of departure for the formation of language but the end to which this process conducts; it is not its *terminus a quo* but its *terminus ad quem*. Language does not enter into a world of objective perceptions already achieved in advance, simply to add to given individual objects signs that would be purely exterior and arbitrary. It is itself a mediator in the formation of objects; it is in one sense the mediator *par excellence*, the most important and valuable instrument for the conquest and construction of a true world of objects (Cassirer 1933, p. 23; cf. Saussure 1966 [1915]; Boas 1965 [1911]; Lévi-Strauss 1966; Douglas 1973).

Once again in this sense, culture is properly understood as an intervention in nature rather than the self-mediation of the latter through symbols. And the biological givens, such as human mating and other facts of life, come into play as instruments of the cultural project, not as its imperatives.

I am making no more claim for culture relative to biology than biology would assert relative to physics and chemistry. In a modern classic on adaptation, G. C. Williams observes that biology is physics and chemistry plus natural selection. But the last is uniquely the principle of matter in living form, and the only one that can account for the *biological* properties of the class of living things. Williams writes,

If asked to explain the trajectory of a falling apple, given an adequate description of its mechanical properties and its initial position and velocity, we would find the principles of mechanics sufficient for a satisfying explanation. They would be as adequate for the apple as for a rock; the living state of the apple would not make this problem biological. If, however, we were asked how the apple acquired its various properties, and why it has these properties instead of others, we would need the theory of natural selection, at least by implication. Only thus could we explain why the apple has a waterproof wax on the outside, and not elsewhere, or why it contains dormant embryos and not something else. . . .

The same story could be told for every normal part or activity of every stage in the life history of every species in the biota of the earth, past or present" (Williams 1966, pp. 5–6).

In the same vein, one might add that gravity constitutes a limit to biological forms: every stage in the life history of every species has to conform to it, and any mutation that might seek structurally to do otherwise does so at its peril. But a limit is only a negative determination; it does not positively specify how the constraint is realized. Within the limits of gravity, every stage of every species has developed; hence such limits explain nothing of the *differentia specifica* of life forms, but only the failure of any of them to exceed certain tolerances. Going still farther, it is possible to say that physical or chemical properties, such as gravity, are means employed by biological forms in the production of the organism. Yet which physical means are employed to what ends—that is, the definite structure of the organism—is uniquely accounted for by natural selection and cannot be stipulated by the laws of inorganic matter. In such a hierarchy of determinations, physical and chemical laws stand as absolutely necessary for the explanation of biological phenomena, but they are equally and absolutely insufficient.

The same kind of hierarchical relationship holds for culture vis-à-vis biology (and by implication, physics and chemistry). Culture is biology plus the symbolic faculty. If we were to ask how a given system of kinship, chieftainship, or religious beliefs acquired its properties, we would have to have a theory of symbolic attribution. Or to take the same old apple: if asked to explain why it had waterproof wax on the outside or why it contained dormant embryos, the principles of natural selection would be sufficient for a satisfying explanation. But if we wanted to know why this fruit and not some other was the sign of carnal knowledge and its consumption the source of the original sin, we would need a theory of meaning. In a recent interview given to the *Harvard Crimson*, E. O. Wilson is quoted as disclaiming any attempt to account biologically for the whole of human social life. Perhaps only 10 percent, he says, can be laid to biology. It is difficult to envision what kind of Modern Synthesis of the social sciences Wilson proposes to establish on a 10 percent margin. But the retreat, if it is one, is not enough. In human cultural behavior, we are not dealing with a multifactorial or overdetermined system into which several considerations of different order and nature enter in certain determinable proportions: a compound of 10 percent biology, 5 percent physics, 3 percent chemistry, 0.7 percent geology, 0.3 percent the action of heavenly bodies and 81 percent the symbolic logic. All of the organic and inorganic constraints are in some sense 100 percent involved: in the sense that cultural life must conform to natural laws. But a law of nature stands to a fact of culture only as a limit does to a form, a constant to a difference, and a matrix to a practice. It will never be possible to explain the cultural properties of any such fact by referring it to underlying contents of a different order.

How then does biology figure in culture? In the least interesting ways as a set of natural limits on human functioning. Most critically, human biology puts at the disposition of culture a set of means for the construction of a symbolic order. One of the best documented examples is color perception (Berlin and Kay 1969). I have elsewhere commented on the problem of color universals in some detail (Sahlins 1976a); here I would involve only the conclusions of that study as they relate to the issue at hand. First, it has to be understood that basic color terms, such as "red," "black," "blue," do not "mean" the indexical act of singling out some segment or chip on a Munsell color chart. As Wittgenstein said, "Point to the color of something—How did you do that?" Colors in cultures are semiotic codes: they are used to signify the differences between life and death, noble and commoner, pure and impure; they distinguish moieties and clans, directions of the compass and the exchange values of two otherwise similar strings of beads. They are engaged as signs in vast schemes of social relations. Now it is exactly because colors subserve this cultural significance that only certain precepts biologically available to human beings become "basic," namely those that by their distinctive contrasts and perceptual relations, such as uniqueness or complementarity of hue, can function as signifiers in meaningful systems. The problem is the same here as in the biological constraints on the types of sound features sufficiently contrastive to be phonemically implemented. The point is that if "yellow" is to be differentiated semantically from "red," the latter is unlikely to be indexically identified as some kind of orange, i.e., on pain of evident contradiction between conceptual and perceptual relations, since one can see both yellow and red in orange. The most salient "red" will be the one on the spectral range that the human eye sees as unique, unmixed with any other color. It is not, then, that color terms have their meanings imposed by the constraints of human and physical nature, as some have suggested; it is that they take on such constraints insofar as they are meaningful.

The structure of human perception provides the natural givens of a cultural project, notably in this case the chromatically unique and complementary pairs of red and green, yellow and blue. But how then shall we account for the presence in cultures of universal biological structures that are not universally present? The range of basic color terms in natural languages is from two to eleven. (I do not know if there are any zero cases; there appear to be none of only one basic term, but minimally two, the panchromatic "light" and "dark," which indicates that the capacity to signal meaningful contrasts is the *raison d'être* of a basic color set.) Clearly cultures are at liberty to variously implement color distinctions as semiotic codes. They are also at liberty to implement the various structures of perceptual contrast that can be devised from the series of basic colors. And most important, they are free to invest colors with their particular meanings, which differ in content from one society to another. We have to deal with a *hierarchical* relation between culture and nature. Like Hegel's cunning of Reason, the wisdom of the cultural process consists in putting to the service of its own intentions natural systems which have their own reasons.

Part Two

Biology and Ideology

III
Ideological Transformations of "Natural Selection"

The evolution of society fits the Darwinian paradigm in its most individualistic form. Nothing in it cries out to be otherwise explained. The economy of nature is competitive from beginning to end. Understand that economy, and how it works, and the underlying reasons for social phenomena are manifest. They are the means by which one organism gains some advantage to the detriment of another. No hint of genuine charity ameliorates our vision of society, once sentimentalism has been laid aside. What passes for cooperation turns out to be a mixture of opportunism and exploitation. The impulses that lead one animal to sacrifice himself for another turn out to have their ultimate rationale in gaining advantage over a third; and acts "for the good" of one society turn out to be performed to the detriment of the rest. Where it is in his own interest, every organism may reasonably be expected to aid his fellows. Where he has no alternative, he submits to the yoke of communal servitude. Yet given a full chance to act in his own interest, nothing but expediency will restrain him from brutalizing, from maiming, from murdering—his brother, his mate, his parent, or his child. Scratch an "altruist," and watch a "hypocrite" bleed (Ghiselin 1974, p. 247).

The Darwinian concept of natural selection has suffered a serious ideological derailment in recent years. Elements of the economic theory of action appropriate to the competitive market have been progressively substituted for the "opportunistic" strategy of evolution envisioned in the 1940s and 1950s by Simpson, Mayr, J. Huxley, Dobzansky, and others. It might be said that Darwinism, at first appropriated to society as "social Darwinism," has returned to biology as a genetic capitalism. Sociobiology has especially contributed to the final stages of this theoretical development. In the earlier stages, the economic principle of "optimization" or "maximization" replaced "differential reproduction" as the fundamental process of natural selection. No distinction is usually made in biology between "optimization" and "maximization": they are used interchangeably as synonyms; although, in other disciplines "optimization" is often contrasted to "maximization" as the one best allocation of resources under the circumstances differs from an ideal strategy of gain independently of circumstances (i.e., as a "perfect" realization of functioning). In either case, this new reading of natural selection has a different calculus of evolutionary advantage than did the traditional idea of "differential reproduction." In an important sense, the latter is a principle of *minimum* significant difference; that is, any consistent advantage in breeding of at least one more offspring that is coded in the genotype of one or more organisms will be positively selected over the other genotypes of the population. We shall see that in the newer form of argument, selection indeed has lost its orienting power in favor of the maximization scheme of the individual biological subject. The structure of this argument transforms selection into the *means* by which DNA optimizes itself over the course of the generations. The orienting force of evolution is thus transferred from external life conditions to the organism itself. In the last stages of ideological derailment, sociobiology conceives the selective strategy—insofar as it is played out in social interactions—as the appropriation of other organisms' life powers to one's own reproductive benefit. Natural selection is ultimately transformed from the appropriation of natural resources to the expropriation of others' resources.

As I say, sociobiology contributes primarily to the final translation of natural selection into social exploitation. For the most part it merely assumes as base the earlier concepts of maximization, which had been taken up by adversaries of "group selection" in support of the alternative of "individual selection," and in any case have a fairly long history in biology. Among sociobiologists, the acceptance of an optimization logic may be more or less nuanced, and the attachment to selection as exploitation likewise varies. The position of Ghiselin cited above is both explicit and extreme. E. O. Wilson, since he allows for the possibility of group selection under certain circumstances, accordingly tempers his adoption of the economic calculus. The position of other sociobiologists, such as Alexander and Trivers, shall be discussed in due course. It is important to note that as a group (Ghiselin excepted), the sociobiologists are rather unselfconscious—and sometimes, apparently, unconscious—about their transfer of utilitarian economic metaphors to the animal kingdom. Occasionally the practice of cost/benefit analysis is rationalized as merely a convenient manner of speaking (Trivers 1972). At the same time, the older conceptions of natural selection as differential reproduction are often accorded explicit deference in sociobiological writing, for no real distinction is seen between differential advantage and maximization, or between environmental fitness and the ability to take advantage of conspecifics. All of these are so many modalities of competition between organisms, hence of natural selection. I take this conflation of contrasting positions, some of them implicit and some explicit, as evidence of the penetration of the biological theory of selection by the folk theory of action.

Essentially, the process of ideological penetration can be divided into two broad phases corresponding to successive appropriations by biology of the mentality of simple commodity production—where producers control their own labor and resources—and that of a fully developed capitalism. But in order to understand these transformations, it will be necessary first to go back to the traditional base of "differential reproduction."

Traditionally, natural selection has been a local principle of historical change. It is defined by specific space and time coordinates, but it is also specifically indeterminate as a principle of gain or fitness. "Positive selection" is any relative advantage maintained by some organism in the ability to produce fertile offspring that is due to a genetically based fitness in dealing with the prevailing environmental circumstances. The effect will be an increased representation of the successful genes in subsequent generations, and so a change in the distribution of gene frequencies for the population as a whole—so long as the selective conditions hold. Nothing is thus asserted about maximization. In the science of economics, it is true that there is only one appropriate answer to any problem of resource allocation: "the one best answer," gain *optimus maxi-*

mus, the particular distribution of resources which maximizes utilities from the means in hand. But natural selection is not *the* one best; it need be only *one* better. In that sense it is a minimum principle. Selection becomes positive the moment any relative advantage is produced. It is not theoretically stipulated that the advantage over conspecifics be the greatest possible. If I have five children, and all my descendants do likewise, while the rest of the population is producing four apiece, sooner or later the genes responsible for this relative success will predominate, so long as the population continues to operate under the same environmental conditions. Of course, if I have eight fertile offspring relative to my associates' four, the predominance will come sooner rather than later, but selection is positive whatever my relative advantage and at the minimum when I have five. If in a game of five-card stud poker I am dealt a pair of kings in every hand, over the long course I will go home the sole winner; albeit, if I hold a flush every hand, the evening is likely to end rather abruptly. Selection is not *in principle* the maximization of individual fitness but any relative advantage whatsoever, becoming positive in sign at the minimum relative difference.

It is thus important to note that while selection may specify a direction of change, it does not specify the final outcome (Levins unpublished). The phenotypical traits representing greater genetic fitness will spread in the population, but this does not of selective necessity entail that these traits will continue to improve or be perfected to the point of structural and functional optimization. For this kind of orthogenetic trend to occur, it would be necessary to suppose further conditions which are neither of the definition of selection nor empirically

probable: most commonly, that the selective circumstances that make the traits in question adaptive
will persist for a time sufficient to allow the required
genetic changes to take place. But again, the principle of selection does not stipulate that the environment (selective pressures) will remain constant for
any given time, let alone a time sufficient for opti-
mum genetic "tracking." It merely stipulates that
during the time the environment holds, the traits
conferring a fitness advantage will tend to prevail.
It is theoretically unwarranted to suggest—as Wilson
(1975, p. 156) and many other biologists seem prone
to do—that it can be predicted (or expected) that
natural selection will favor the maximization of this
or that structural change or functional capacity.
In any such statement, "natural selection" always
means 'natural selection plus one or more other and
implicit assumptions.' Once more, selection is a local
principle of directional change, acting positively on
any measure of relative fitness for a particular environment during the particular period of time this
environment persists.

If the selective pressures change in character,
so does the coefficient of fitness and the direction
of adaptive change. This is one of the senses of the
received understanding that evolution is "opportunistic." (Another, it might be noted, is that dif-
ferentiation and the exploitation of new niches is
likely to be more favored than a tactic of directional
change, insofar as the success of the latter has to
be won against direct competition within the species.)
But the fundamental motivation of the concept of
"opportunism" was the indeterminancy of the primary sources of evolutionary change, genetic and
environmental variation. More exactly, these variations have no necessary relation to each other.

Mutation (or chromosome recombination) is a chance event relative to the selective conditions: generated by a biological dynamic independent of the environment, it is normally deleterious to the organisms involved. Nor do environmental changes proceed out of regard for the fitness of the life forms which may be affected. Except for some suggestions about selective pressure on the rate of mutation, such understandings of the mechanics of evolutionary change appear still to be the commonplace wisdom of biology. What they clearly imply is that *indeterminancy*, not maximization, is of the *nature* of evolutionary change. How did we get the idea that "natural selection" is a process of maximization?

Part of the answer was offered in chapter 2. Out of the criticism of "group selection" came a redoubled insistence on "individual selection"; and in opposition to the "altruism" of the former came the "egotism" of the latter. The emphasis on egotism made it easy to slip logically from the differential reproduction of organisms to a competition between them, from competition to self-maximization, and, in sociobiology, from the maximization of the self to the exploitation of others. All of these became so many synonyms for each other and for "natural selection." Yet as we have also noticed already, the internal dialectics of biology are insufficient to account for the transformation of selection into these several species of maximization. This may be documented by the very important inconsistencies that still attend biologists' views on maximization.

It cannot be claimed that either group selectionists or sociobiologists are unremitting in their invocation of "maximization." On the contrary, they are very well aware of the indeterminacies of the traditional theory. "No organism is ever perfectly adapted," writes Wilson, "nearly all the relevant parameters of its environment shift constantly" (1975, p. 144). Biologists recognize that selection typically is not and cannot be maximizing if only because something short of that is introduced by "selective compromises," "phylogenetic inertia," or linkages in the organic structure which may limit development in certain directions or induce allometric distortions in others. To be *aware* of something, however, to *recognize* it, is not the same thing as knowing the *concept* of it. It is not to put it in its right theoretical place. The concept of natural selection generally adopted in sociobiology is maximization, as in statements of the theory of kin selection or of parent-offspring conflict. Now as the people involved are all serious and brilliant biological scholars, this inconsistency between their concept of maximization and their awareness of opportunism implies that something is going on which is not entirely motivated by positive biology. But then, biology is not practiced in a social vacuum. It is a specialized intellectual activity within a society of given historic type. Without alleging any political intentions, it would not be surprising ethnographically to find in the contradictions of biology's conception of gain the symptom of its dual cultural existence. Especially as it turned to the study of society itself, it would not be immune to the ideology of the marketplace. All of Western science ridiculed the biology of Lysenko. Could something like that happen here?

Consider the following propositions about natural selection asserted by group selectionists and sociobiologists.

G. Williams writes, "the reproduction of every individual is designed to maximize the number of its successful offspring" (1966, p. 132). Again: "the various aspects of the reproductive behavior and physiology of a species, its intensity, timing, ontogeny, and every important feature of its physiological and behavioral mechanisms would be precisely designed to maximize individual reproductive performance" (ibid., pp. 191–92). Williams cites Medawar's characterization of "fitness" with certain reserves, but these apparently do not extend to Medawar's conflation of evolutionary processes with market economics:

> The genetical use of "fitness" is an extreme attenuation of ordinary usage [*mais, au contraire!*]: it is, in effect, a system of pricing the endowments of organisms in the currency of offspring, i.e., in terms of net reproductive performance. It is a genetic valuation of goods, not a statement about their nature or quality (ibid., p. 158).

The following passage of E. O. Wilson's is useful to illustrate the further transformations imposed on evolutionary theory. Here the organism becomes the self-directing subject of change, and selection enters as the instrumental means of its perfection:

> When exploratory behavior leads one or a few animals to a breakthrough enhancing survival and reproduction, the capacity for that kind of exploratory behavior and the imitation of the successful act are favored by natural selection. The enabling portions of the anatomy, particularly the brain, will then be perfected by evolution (Wilson 1975, p. 156).

Recall Wilson's dictum that no organism is ever perfectly adapted, because "nearly all the relevant

parameters of its environment shift constantly."
In any case, here is Trivers on maximum net returns:

> For a given reproductive season one can de-
> fine the total parental investment of an indi-
> vidual as the sum of its investments in each of
> its offspring produced during that season, and
> one assumes that natural selection has favored
> the parental investment that leads to maximum
> net reproductive success (1972, p. 139).

Alexander's views on selection are useful in
illustrating the development of the concept to the
level of the full market system where (capital) reproduction proceeds through an exchange that pro-
curs for itself the labor power of others:

> From the evolutionist's point of view, two prin-
> ciples must be recognized. First, all organisms
> are assumed to be evolving continually to maxi-
> mize their own inclusive fitness. Second, the
> giving of benefits of any kind to another organ-
> ism always involves expense, however slight,
> to the beneficent. This response includes a fit-
> ness reduction because of time and energy con-
> sumed, and risks taken. It also involves a rela-
> tive fitness reduction resulting from the increase
> in fitness of the reproductively competitive
> recipient. Thus, all organisms should have
> evolved to avoid every instance of beneficence
> or altruism unlikely to bring returns greater
> than the expenditure it entails (1975, p. 90; cf.
> 1974).

This is merely a very small sample of a very
large phenomenon. It would be easy to accumulate

many more examples, but more useful to analyze a few characteristic arguments. For the serious question is, by what structure of argument are chance events such as genetic and environmental shifts nonetheless conceived to maximize the selective outcome? Consider the biological tale of why the Pacific salmon lays so many eggs at once. As it happens, both Williams and Wilson offer the same kind of explanation for this phenomenon. It seems to be the fair average biological reasoning in such cases. The argument can be described as a method for reintroducing the traditional bugbear of teleology into adaptation by arbitrarily taking certain functions and/or structures of an existing organism as a priori, in some way given and earlier, so that the adaptive problem is then set by the organism, viz., by the necessity to render the given systems more effective. Structures or activities complementary to those already given are then seen as having been favored in the subsequent course of evolution, that is, by virtue of their contributions to the a priori fitness demands. A systematic organism has been temporalized analytically into earlier and later parts, which accords its project of maximization the role of orienting force of evolution and engages natural selection as a *means* put at the disposition of the organic subject. Said another way, then, "phylogenetic inertia" becomes the decisive force of evolution.

So it is taken as given that the salmon, after a long and debilitating swim upstream, will spawn only once. That being the case, it becomes selectively favorable that she lay as many eggs as possible, even though it kills her, to maximize the chances of leaving viable offspring. "The Pacific salmons spawn only once, and among them we find the expected emphasis on reproductive functions to the detriment of the parental soma" (Williams 1966, p. 174). Consequently, we also find that before her heroic spawning run to death and immortality at once, the salmon undergoes certain organic changes that optimize her egg-bearing capacity, such as atrophy of the digestive system. Although these changes make her own continued existence impossible, they are positively adaptive (selected for), as, for example, by their provision of materials and space for an increased number of gametes (ibid.). In other words, taking the fact of single spawning as inevitable, it is sensible that evolution proceed to maximize the reproductive tract at the expense of the digestive. Wilson offers essentially the same problematic in the characteristic terms of an entrepreneurial calculus:

For a given reproductive effort θj made at any age j, there is a profit to be measured in the number of offspring produced. There is also a cost to be measured in the lowered survival probability at age j and subsequent ages. The cost consists in the investment in energy and time, together with the reduced reproductive potential at later ages, due to the slowed growth in turn caused by the effect θj. How would a profit function form a concave curve and thus favor semelparity? If a female salmon laid only one or two eggs, the reproductive effort, consisting principally of the long swim upstream, would be very high. To lay hundreds more eggs entails only a small amount of additional reproductive effort (1975, p. 97).

As a representation of natural selection, the fallacy of this reasoning, which might be called "the fallacy of an a priori fitness course," is fairly evident. The several difficulties are summed up by the question, if selection will go so far as to atrophy the digestive tract in favor of a single reproductive explosion that also kills the organism, why should it not as easily effect structural changes that will allow the salmon to spawn twice or more to the same fitness effect, as for instance sturgeons do? (cf. ibid., p. 95). The problem is that this course or some other was precluded not by a natural selection but by an analytic one. The salmon was taken as an a priori limited being with only one possible solution to the evolutionary problem of resource allocation to fitness, by a premise not motivated in the nature of evolution itself. The salmon is going to have only one chance to lay eggs, and that at very considerable cost. Once this set of conditions is taken as given, all other evolutionary possibilities to the same net fitness effect may be conveniently ignored. Since they are ignored, selection enters into the explanation as the mode of achieving an outcome intrinsic to the salmon. And the salmon's self-determined project of maximization becomes the logic of adaptive change. In other words, by the nature of the argument, the roles of the organism and natural selection in traditional evolutionary theory are perfectly reversed: the organism sets the orientation of change, while selection is assigned the function of providing the necessary materials.

In an important article on "reciprocal altruism" by Trivers (1971), also substantially relied upon by Wilson (1975), this kind of fascination with individual net gain becomes so overwhelming that it actually prevails over differential advantage between individuals as the definition of selection. Selection is held to occur whenever the individual derives net benefits from social interaction, despite that these benefits may entail no advantage whatsoever over others of the group. The self-contradictions of Trivers's argument and the adoption of the same by Wilson are in fact interrelated phenomena. For what the argument thus affords is an air-tight case for sociobiology whereby both altruistic action that confers no relative advantage to the altruist and action that does (as in kin selection) may be equally considered "adaptive," the latter now simply defined as net (rather than relative) gain. L. Allen, B. Beckwith, et al. of the Boston-Cambridge Sociobiology Study Group (1976 unpublished), have reasonably criticized the procedure on the positivist grounds that it cannot then be tested: theory "will always lead to a non-falsifiable adaptive story." This is perfectly true: if ego is good to his kinsmen, it benefits his own inclusive fitness; if, on the other hand, he aids a stranger rather than a kinsman, it also comes back to his advantage in the form of a reciprocal altruism. Still, something remains to be discovered about Trivers's argument, for whenever we are thus confronted by two different hypotheses that purport to account for contradictory phenomena by one and the same principle, it is certain that the hypotheses themselves contradict each other.

Trivers argues that reciprocal altruism will as effectively as kin selection promote individual fitness benefits. He begins with an example that in some respects (though not decisive ones) is unfortunate. If you were to save a drowning man who without your help would have a 50 percent chance of dying, this at the small risk to your own mortality (and his too in this case) of say 5 percent; and if at some future time he were to save you from a similar plight, when the respective chances of living and dying were reversed, i.e., you now had a 50 percent chance, he had a 5 percent risk, then you (as well as he) would have increased your chances of surviving over the long run, by some 40 percent. (I say the example is unfortunate because after all it would be evolutionarily short-sighted to save a man who can't swim on the supposition that he will later rescue you from drowning, and because you might reasonably calculate that his chances of saving you in the future are something less than 50 percent, which is the best he can do for himself. But of course, no serious matter: it would be easy to think of better examples.) Trivers goes on to propose that any set of organisms that was genetically prepared to so cooperate with each other would not only do so because individually each thereby increases his life chances, but would also spread their reciprocal-altruist genes in the population at the expense of those who did not see fit(ness) to cooperate. It is important to note that such advantage is gained not by the individual altruists vis-à-vis each other, but by the group of reciprocators in relation to nonparticipating members of the community. Hence it is the bond between organisms who do not genetically compete with each other, i.e., who individually settle for parity with certain genetic competitors, that yields the selective advantage. Eventually this group should constitute the entire population. With an eye singular to the individual profit, however, Trivers supposes that, "No concept of group advantage is necessary to explain the function of human altruistic behavior" (1971, p. 48).

Having established this population of reciprocating organisms without any recourse to kin selection, or as he believes group selection, Trivers then adduces for humans a number of individual psychological and social dispositions that would follow on evolutionary principles. At this point, both action which yields differential benefits to individuals *and action which does not* become equally and indiscriminately adaptive. For the dispositions adduced are either selected for as means of compelling others to enter into reciprocity, or as counteracting the temptations of others to "cheat" on reciprocal obligations—temptations also adaptive, since they effect an individual net gain through exploitation. Thus Trivers purports to account biologically for such human tendencies as sympathy, guilt, gratitude, friendliness, self-righteousness, and moral aggression, as well as the ability to dissimulate any of these, in the adaptive interest of inducing reciprocity, holding exchange partners to their obligations or else escaping their adaptive efforts to employ sanctions on any ego's adaptive inclinations to cheat. For example: "Once strong positive emotions have evolved to motivate altruistic behavior, the altruist is in a vulnerable position because cheaters will be selected to take advantage of the altruist's positive emotions. This in turn sets up a selection pressure for a protective mechanism. Moralistic aggression and indignation in humans was selected for . . ." (ibid., p. 49). The system of relations, in other words, is in a constant movement to effect a reciprocal equilibrium in the face of an equally constant threat of unbalance, both of which are from different viewpoints advantageous tendencies.

The last part of Trivers's argument is marked by an extreme ethnocentrism: the conception that reciprocity develops and is organized by a free-market traffic in benefits; the supposition that it is generally attended in human groups by such attitudes as gratitude, friendliness, self-righteousness, or moral aggression—there are any number of ethnographic examples to the contrary; and by the heavy reliance on tests of the psychological dispositions of Western subjects as evidence of what "humans" do. Of course it is true that all Americans are human, but it is not true that all humans are American—and still less that all animals are Americans. One is reminded of Rousseau's dictum that if you want to study men, look about you, but if you want to study Man it will be necessary to go abroad, for it is only by observing the differences that one can discover the properties (cf. Langer 1971). Yet ethnocentrism is not the decisive point. The decisive point is that Trivers becomes so interested in the fact that in helping others one helps himself, he forgets that in so doing one also benefits genetic competitors as much as oneself, so that in all moves that generalize a reciprocal balance, no *differential* (let alone optimal) advantage accrues to this so-called adaptive activity. In the name of adaptation, the virtue attributed to the development of reciprocal altruism is that it eliminates differential individual advantage all along the line. Hence the apparent nonfalsifiability of the argument: both altruism and nonaltruism are gainful, thus "adaptive"—so long as one does not inquire further whether the gain is also relative to other organisms.

Actually, what Trivers produces is a very good model of "group selection" or as it might better be called, "social selection." In this model, moreover, the unit of selection is not the individual organism, nor strictly speaking is it the group, but certain *social relations* into which individuals enter in pursuing their own lives. These relations may not confer any differential advantages to these individuals taken separately. But they do advantage the group or subgroup practicing them, thus indirectly the individuals participating in them, vis-à-vis others of the species who might be incapable of entertaining the relations in question. Even for the biological study of animal social organization, it will be necessary to take a "superorganic" perspective. Meanwhile, as for the biology of reciprocal altruism, the perspective of sociobiology collapses under the contradiction that such generalized altruism yields no *differential* benefits in individual fitness. At the same time, the ideological source of sociobiology's concept of selection is rather dramatically revealed. "Selection" is reduced to individual net profit, pure and simple, since not even the relative advantage over conspecifics is necessary to the definition of the term.

"Reciprocal altruism" as Trivers views it is an economics of petty commercial exchange.[1] In another important article on "Parental Investment and Sexual Selection" (1972), Trivers introduces a more advanced form of economic relationships between individuals. Here each is engaged in a struggle to turn the labor of others to his own account. The outlook is no longer petty bourgeois: we are in a developed capitalist economy. Again Trivers is hardly concerned to show any differential advantages. Or rather, natural selection comes down to the one kind of advantage involved in increasing one's own reproductive success by appropriating the life powers of others. It is not a question either of relative fitness in relation to the exploitation of environmental resources. The scarce resources of evolutionary change exist in other members of the species so that natural selection becomes synonymous with social exploitation.

The article is mostly about birds. As usual, it does have an eye toward the "human" implications.

(Thus, "Elder [1969] shows that steady dating and sexual activity [coitus and petting] in adolescent *human* females correlate inversely with a tendency to marry up the socioeconomic economic scale as adults" p. 146; italics added.) The argument is complex, devoted to showing the relation between variations in "parental investment" of the sexes and sexual selection. I single out here only a portion of the material relevant to the present discussion. Trivers's general thesis rests on the observation of an inverse relation between the relative investment of any one sex in parental care and the amount of competition within that sex for mates. The reasoning is that if, for example, all parental and postnatal investment falls on the female, the effect will be to reduce her capacity for rearing offspring over a lifetime. Since the costs for the males, however, consist only in insemination, and they can thus produce a great many offspring, females become a scarce reproductive resource and in proportion the subject of an intense competition. One should bear in mind—as Trivers's failure to deploy the fact is a source of inadequacy in his thesis—that the intrasexual competition will also proportionately increase the mortality chances of the sex investing less in offspring.

The inadequacy consist in this: Trivers invites us to consider the moment in time when the offspring are just hatched, the male having contributed nothing but the costs of sexual exercise while the female has had to invest substantially in the chicks while *in utero*. (The assumption, incidentally, is the functional version of "the fallacy of an a priori fitness course," as in the Pacific salmon.) At this particular conjuncture, a male will be sorely tempted to desert, leaving the female to rear the brood as best she can, which she may very well be inclined to do in order to amortize an already considerable investment. Any success the female might have will be also to the male's reproductive advantage, as she is rearing his offspring; while in the meantime, he can increase his fitness still further by promiscuous adventures with such other females as he can secure. Apparently reasonable, this calculation on Trivers's part contains a minor flaw as well as a major one. The minor problem is sexist. It is hardly to the female's advantage to put up with this neglect of herself and her offspring, and Trivers in fact indicates that females should be selected to effect a degree of male parental care (as through judging male inclinations in courtship displays). The major inadequacy ensues from Trivers's neglect to figure into the calculus the increased mortality chances among males that his theory predicts for a situation of limited male investment, scarce female resources, and correspondingly intense competition among promiscuous males. There is no showing on Trivers's part that the reproductive advantages of desertion for the male are any greater than fitness losses he is liable to incur in competition—not to mention that abandonment of his one-time consort reduces her chances of raising his offspring. Without additional assumptions or observations, there is no basis at all for supposing that this kind of exploitation of females maximizes the individual male's reproduction, hence is "selected for." And insofar as any degree of male parental investment reduces the risks of competition, even as it increases the life chances of the offspring, neither is there a basis for supposing that any degree of "monogamy" or "promiscuity" (passing by way of occasional "adultery") is more advantageous than any other. In fact, most birds are monogamous. Trivers exemplifies these several types of mating among diverse avian species. But no one type can recommend itself over the others on grounds of reproductive self-interest. For as males "invest" more, they may breed less, but they and young will live longer. Trivers's argument from maximization is—if the pun can be forgiven—specious.[2]

What the argument does show is the final degeneration of evolutionary biology to native ideology. Already burdened with the notion of maximization, "natural selection," when transposed to the level of behavior, becomes a familiar language of social exploitation. In the next chapter, I will show more particularly how successive reformulations of the concept of selection correspond to successive stages of capitalism. But it needs no elaborate demonstration to see already why sociobiology, by completing this ideological progression, becomes a subject of political contention—whether intentionally or not, it doesn't matter.

IV

Folk Dialectics of Nature and Culture

> So that in the first place, I put for a generall in-
> clination of all mankind, a perpetuall and restlesse
> desire of Power after power, that ceaseth onely in
> Death.
>
> THOMAS HOBBES, *Leviathan*

To discover the lineaments of the larger society in the concepts of its biology is not altogether a "Modern Synthesis." In Euro-American society this integration has been going on in a particular dialectic way since the seventeenth century. Since Hobbes, at least, the competitive and acquisitive characteristics of Western man have been confounded with Nature, and the Nature thus fashioned in the human image has been in turn reapplied to the explanation of Western man. The effect of this dialectic has been to anchor the properties of human social action, as we conceive them, in Nature, and the laws of Nature in our conceptions of human social action. Human society is natural, and natural societies are curiously human. Adam Smith produces a social version of Thomas Hobbes, Charles Darwin a naturalized version of Adam Smith; William Graham Sumner thereupon reinvents Darwin as society, and Edward O. Wilson reinvents Sumner as nature. Since

Darwin, the movement of the conceptual pendulum has accelerated. Every decade, it seems, we are presented with a more refined notion of man as species, and a more refined species of "natural selection" as man.

In the opening chapters of *Leviathan* there is presented a picture of man as a self-moving and self-directing machine. C. B. Macpherson, whose reading of Hobbes and explication of "possessive individualism" I here follow very closely, describes the Hobbesian natural man as an "automated machine," having built into it "equipment by which it alters its motion in response to differences in the material it uses, and to the impact and even the expected impact of other matter on it" (1962, p. 31). The machine is part of the informational system of the world in which it moves, as nothing is present to its mind that was not first present to its senses— "there is no conception in a man's mind, which hath not at first, totally, or by parts, been begotten by the organs of sense" (Hobbes, part 1, chap. 1; all citations of *Leviathan* are from the Everyman Paperback edition [1950]). Language introduces the potentiality of error into this sensory epistemology, as also a greater capacity for right movements, but it cannot transcend the intrinsic values of sensory experience. In chapters 5 through 11, the general direction of the machine is indicated. "Felicity of this life," Hobbes says, "consisteth not in the repose of a mind satisfied. . . . Nor can a man any more live, whose Desires are at an end. . . . Felicity is a continuall progresse of the desire" (chap. 11). The machine acts to continue its own motion by approaching things that sustain that motion and avoiding things inimical. Motion toward is "desire" (or "appetite") and its objects are "good." Motion away is "aversion" and its objects are "evil." Each human machine "endeavoureth to secure himselfe against the evill he feares, and procure the good he desireth" (chap. 12). As the abstract positive and negative of human action, these two motions are comprehensive. They exhaust all particular motivations which are just so many circumstantial modalities of motion toward or motion away. Appetite with the opinion it will be satisfied is "hope"; without this opinion "despair." Aversion with the anticipation of hurt from the object is "fear"; with the hope of resisting hurt, it is "courage." And so for anger, confidence, diffidence, indignation, benevolence, covetousness, pusillanimity and magnanimity, liberality and parsimony, kindness, lust or jealousy—they are products of a single-minded concern for one's own good.

In the eighth chapter, however, Hobbes states the relativity of the calculus of good. Insofar as it is social, it is a differential good. Hobbes argues that the good men value is determined by whatever other men already have. Virtue and worth are only realizable as a differential success, as preeminence, and "consisteth in comparison. For if all things were equally in all men, nothing would be prized" (chap. 8). The success of men in securing their own good thus depends on the strength of their desires and their respective abilities. But then, the pursuit of one's own good cannot remain at the level of independent production. For the power of one man to obtain his own good is opposed by the powers of others. "The power of one man resisteth and hindereth the effects of the power of another" (cf. Macpherson 1962, pp. 35–36). There is an opposition of powers. And in the end, success turns on the competitive appropriation of the powers of others. A man secures his own good to the extent he can harness the powers of other men. There is a net transfer of powers. The means are all such things as riches, reputation, love, and fear. "Riches joyned with liberality, is Power; because it procureth friends, and servants. . . . Reputation of Power, is Power; because it draweth with it the adhearence of those that need protection. . . . Also, what quality soever maketh a man beloved, or feared of many, or the reputation of such quality, is Power; because it is the means to have the assistance, and service of many" (chap. 10). Macpherson notes that in Hobbes's scheme, men actually enter into a market for the exchange of powers. Men find their worth as the price others will pay for the use of their powers. It is in this mode, as *acquisition*, that Hobbes put as the "generall inclination of all mankind, a perpetuall and restlesse desire of Power after power, that ceaseth onely in Death" (chap. 11). As all men are so inclined, no one man can rest secure in his own powers without engaging "by force, or wiles, to master the persons of all men he can, so long, till he see no other power great enough to endanger him" (chap. 13). Hence the famous struggle among men in a state of nature, the "Warre" of every man against every man, enduring so long as they do not agree to surrender their force to a Common Power (the State) that will "keep them all in awe."

Writing in an era of transition to a developed market society, Hobbes reproduces the historical sequence as a logic of human nature. The expropriation of man by man at which Hobbes arrives in the end is, as Macpherson explains, the theory of action in a fully competitive economy. It differs from a mere struggle for preeminence, as would occur in transitional phases of simple commodity production, because in the model of the latter each man has access to his own means of livelihood and need not convey his powers to other men. Producers may maximize their own position in market exchange; they remain, however, independent proprietors and their labor power as such is not a commodity. The full market system also differs from exploitative structures such as feudalism and slavery, since in the latter conditions, the rights to power, although they may yield a net transfer, are relatively fixed among the classes. No one is free to convey his powers as he will, for none can escape his definition as a social being, definition that presupposes his position in the circulation of powers. Men are slaves and serfs, others are lords and masters, but the system is not competitive such that it would be necessary to struggle after more power just to conserve the amount one has, or else lose out to those stronger in desire or capacity. The full market system refers to the historical time when men do become free to alienate their powers for a price, as some are compelled to do because they lack the productive means to independently realize their own good. This is a very distinctive type of society as well as a particular period of history. It is marked by what Macpherson styles "possessive individualism." Possessive individualism entails the unique notion—counterpart to the liberation from feudal relations—that men own their own bodies, the use of which they have both the freedom and necessity to sell to those who control their own capital. (It was Marx, of course, who penetrated the inequities of this exchange, that is, the net transfer, since the value produced by labor power is greater than its price.) In such a condition, every man confronts every man as an owner. Indeed, society itself is generated through the acts of exchange by which each seeks the greatest possible

benefits in others' powers at the least possible cost
to his own.

It was, Macpherson explains,

> a conception of the individual as essentially the
> proprietor of his own person or capacities, ow-
> ing nothing to society for them. The individual
> was seen neither as a moral whole, nor as part
> of a larger social whole, but as owner of him-
> self. The relation of ownership, having become
> for more and more men the critically important
> relation in determining their actual freedom and
> actual prospect of realizing their full potentiali-
> ties, was read back into the nature of the in-
> dividual. . . . Society becomes a lot of free
> individuals related to each other as proprietors
> of their own capacities and of what they have
> acquired by their exercise. *Society consists of*
> *relations of exchange between proprietors*
> (1962, p. 3; italics added).

Social scientists will recognize in this description the "utilitarianism" that has beset their own
disciplines since Spencer and before (cf. Parsons
1968; Sahlins 1976b). It is precisely a perspective in
which the individual is seen "neither as a moral
whole, nor as part of a larger social whole, but as
owner of himself." In the social sciences, as in sociobiology, the homebred economizing of the market
place is then all too easily transposed from the
analysis of capitalist society to the explication of
society *tout court*. The analytic place thus left to the
social fact has been well described by Louis Dumont:

> In modern society . . . the Human Being is
> regarded as the indivisible, "elementary" man,

both a biological being and a thinking subject. Each particular man in a sense incarnates the whole of mankind. He is the measure of all things (in a full and novel sense). The kingdom of ends coincides with each man's legitimate ends, so the values are turned upside down. What is still called "society" is the means, the life of each man is the end. Ontologically, the society no longer exists, it is no more than an irreducible datum, which must in no way thwart the demands of liberty and equality. Of course, the above is a description of values, a view of mind. . . . A society as conceived by individualism has never existed anywhere for the reason we have given, namely, that the individual lives on social ideas (1970, pp. 9–10).

I underscore Dumont's observations on the indivisibility of the human being in the perspective of the sociological utilitarianism: man as a thinking subject is also the same man as a biological being. Hence society may be derived from the rational action of individuals seeking to satisfy their needs —a project in which "thought" serves merely as the means and the representation of inherent ends. Sociobiology operates on exactly the same premise. Hobbes provided the original basis for this subordination of the symbolic to the natural by situating the society he knew in the state of nature. Man was seen as a wolf to man. Again one can say that the objective of sociobiologists is very similar so far as it concerns human society. But it goes further. Since they would now extend the same folk conception of capitalism to the animal kingdom as a whole, for sociobiologists it is also true that the wolf is a man to other wolves. Actually, however, I compress a long cycle of reciprocal interpretations of nature and culture that has been characteristic of the Western consciousness, both as science and as ideology. I can briefly describe this cycle by making two further points.

First, it is clear that the Hobbesian vision of man in a natural state is the origin myth of Western capitalism. In modern social practice, the story of Genesis pales by comparison. Yet it is also clear that in this comparison, and indeed in comparison with the origin myths of all other societies, the Hobbesian myth has a very peculiar structure, one that continues to attend our understandings of ourselves. So far as I am aware, we are the only society on earth that thinks of itself as having risen from savagery, identified with a ruthless nature. Everyone else believes they are descended from gods. Even if these gods have natural representations, they nonetheless have supernatural attributes. Judging from social behavior, this contrast may well be a fair statement of the differences between ourselves and the rest of the world. In any case we make both a folklore and a science of our brutish origins, sometimes with precious little to distinguish between them. And just as Hobbes believed that the institution of society or the Commonwealth did not abolish the nature of man as wolf to other men but merely permitted its expression in relative safety, so we continue to believe in the savage within us— of which we are slightly ashamed. At an earlier period it was *Homo economicus*, with a natural propensity to truck and barter, an idea that rationalized the developing capitalist society to itself. It took but two centuries to evolve another species, *Homo bellicosus*, or so one might classify that contentious ape popularized by Ardrey and other recent writers.

Now comes sociobiology, and with it apparently a reversion to economic type, programmed in the natural propensity of DNA to maximize itself at the expense of whom it may concern.

Hence the response by men of the Left becomes intelligible, as does the interest of the public at large. What is inscribed in the theory of sociobiology is the entrenched ideology of Western society: the assurance of its naturalness, and the claim of its inevitability.

The second point concerns the ideological dialectic to which I previously alluded. Since the seventeenth century we seem to have been caught up in this vicious cycle, alternately applying the model of capitalist society to the animal kingdom, then reapplying this bourgeoisfied animal kingdom to the interpretation of human society. My intent in adopting the Macpherson reading of Hobbes was just to imply that most of the elements and stages of the biological theory of natural selection—from differential success to the competitive struggle to reproduce one's stock and the transfer of powers—already existed in the *Leviathan*. As a critic of this capitalist conception, it was left to Marx to discern its realization in Darwinian theory. In a letter to Engels, Marx wrote:

> It is remarkable how Darwin recognizes among beasts and plants his English society with its division of labour [read, diversification], competition, opening up of new markets [niches], "inventions" [variations], and the Malthusian "struggle for existence." It is Hobbes's "bellum omnium contra omnes," and one is reminded of Hegel's *Phenomenology* where civil society is described as a "spiritual animal kingdom,"

while in Darwin the animal kingdom figures as civil society (Marx in Schmidt 1971, p. 46).

The same point was to be made later by Hofstadter:

A parallel can be drawn between the patterns of natural selection and classical economics, suggesting that Darwinism involved an addition to the vocabulary rather than to the substance of conventional economic theory. Both assumed the fundamentally self-interested animal pursuing, in the classical pattern, pleasure or, in the Darwinian pattern, survival. Both assumed the normality of competition in the exercise of the hedonistic, or survival, impulse; and in both it was the "fittest," usually in a eulogistic sense, who survived or prospered— either the organism most satisfactorily adapted to his environment, or the most efficient and economic producer, the most frugal and temperate worker (1959, p. 144).

In a letter to Lavrov, Engels described the ensuing dialectical return, the representation of culture to itself in the form of a capitalist nature:

The whole Darwinist teaching of the struggle for existence is simply a transference from society to living nature of Hobbes's doctrine of "bellum omnium contra omnes" and of the bourgeois-economic doctrine of competition together with Malthus's theory of population. When this conjurer's trick has been performed . . . the same theories are transferred back again from organic nature into history and now it is claimed that their validity as eternal laws of human society has been proved (Engels in Schmidt 1971, p. 47).

It might be noted that Darwin was not altogether happy with this reciprocal reflection of the animal kingdom as his own English society. "I have received in a Manchester newspaper rather a good squib," he wrote to Sir Charles Lyell, "showing that I have proved 'might is right,' and therefore that Napoleon is right, and every cheating tradesman is also right" (cited in Hofstadter 1955, p. 85).

But no such reserve would inhibit William Graham Sumner—to take the outstanding American example—from transferring the Darwinian teaching back to its original social source. "The truth is that the social order is fixed by laws of nature precisely analogous to those of the physical order" (Sumner 1934, vol. 2, p. 107). Hofstadter succinctly summarizes Sumner's inspiration:

> In the Spencerian intellectual atmosphere of the 1870's and 1880's it was natural for conservatives to see the economic contest in competitive society as a reflection of the struggle in the animal world. It was easy to argue by analogy from natural selection of fitter organisms to social selection of fitter men, from organic forms with superior adaptability to citizens with a greater store of economic virtues. . . . The progress of civilization, according to Sumner, depends on the selection process; and that in turn depends upon the workings of unrestricted competition. Competition is a law of nature which "can no more be done away with than gravitation," and which men can ignore only to their sorrow (Hofstadter 1959, p. 57).

One aspect of Sumner's biologism deserves special comment. It concerns the motivation which Sumner frequently alleged for the accumulation of wealth in a ruthless competitive struggle. This is exactly the same motivation adduced by sociobiology for the parallel struggle in nature—"inheritance" (by the offspring of the fittest). The double service of the term is not unusual. From the late Middle Ages onward, Western society has gone to considerable effort to encode its economic activity within a pervasive metaphor of improvement of the stock. Terms for animal reproduction have been appropriated for economic categories and vice versa, at first figuratively, but then so consistently that metaphor dies and it becomes impossible to distinguish the original reference from the derived. The peculiarity of a native category that refers interchangeably to the social reproduction of economic goods and the natural reproduction of animate beings then goes unnoticed, banished from consciousness as well as memory. On the contrary, the category becomes a basis for scientific or popular reflections on the essential identity of the two processes. These reflections accordingly take the form of a folk etymology. They recapitulate, for example, the derivation of the English terms "capital" and "chattel" from an older "cattle," which precisely as the movable and increasable "livestock" was distinguished from the dead stock of fixed farm equipment. (Indeed the common origin of the concepts of transactable wealth and cattle in the Indo-European *peku*, together with the appearance of a cognate category of *pasū viru* in Avestan including men and their domestic animals, suggests a primitive integration of the economic, the social and the natural; modern usage would merely represent a cognitive homology [cf. Benveniste 1969; and relevant entries of the *OED*].) It is the same with "inheritance," which initially referred to the continuity of goods over generations of people, only to denote at a later date the continuity of the generational "stock" itself. W. G. Sumner was thus empowered by the folk wisdom to find cause for the economic competition over resources in a genetic transmission— just as E. O. Wilson would later describe the natural process of genetic transmission as a struggle for resources:

> The socialist assails particularly the institution of bequest or hereditary property. . . . The right of bequest rests on no other grounds than those of expediency. The love of children is the strongest motive to frugality and to the accumulation of capital. The state guarantees the power of bequest only because it thereby encourages the accumulation of capital on which the welfare of society depends . . . hereditary wealth transmitted from generation to generation is the strongest instrument by which we keep up a steadily advancing civilization (Sumner 1934, vol. 2, pp. 112–13).

We seem unable to escape from this perpetual movement, back and forth between the culturalization of nature and the naturalization of culture. It frustrates our understanding at once of society and of the organic world. In the social sciences we exhaust our own symbolic capacities in an endless reproduction of utilitarian theorizing, some of it economic, some ecologic. In the natural sciences, it is the vulgar and scientific sociobiologies. All these efforts taken together represent the modern encompassment of the sciences, both of culture and of life, by the dominant ideology of possessive individualism.

The net effect is a curious form of totemism of which scientific sociobiology is the latest incarnation. For if totemism is, as Lévi-Strauss says, the explication of differences between human groups by reference to the distinctions between natural species, such that clan *A* is related to and distinct from clan *B* as the eagle hawk is to the crow, then sociobiology merits classification as the highest form of the totemic philosophy. For its sophistication and advance over the primitive varieties, both in the West and abroad, it does seem to merit a special name, one in keeping with its own synthetic pretensions as the latest branch of the sciences and the principal hope of civilization. Give it its due: sociobiology is a Scientific Totemism.

But with all respects to the *pensée sauvage*, this reliance on the deep structure of Western thought, with its assimilation of the reproduction of people to the reproduction of goods as a kinship of substance, cannot do for the science to which we now aspire. The confusion of categories is too immoderate. It puts us all, biological and social scientists alike, in the state known all too well to the practitioners of totemism: of mess and "dirt," as Mary Douglas has taught us, of pollution and tabu. Beyond all the politics, it is of course this descent into the kingdom of tabu that ultimately makes sociobiology so fascinating. But we pay a heavy penalty in knowledge for the distinctions we are forced to surrender. "The most serious harm to science that I see in the present fashion of applying ethnological terms to animals," Susan Langer writes, "is that— odd as it may seem—it is really based on the assumption that the two studies, ethnology and what is called 'ethology' . . . will never become true integral parts of biological science. If they should ever do so, the use of words literally in one context and figuratively in another would cause havoc" (1971, p. 328). Yet we stand to lose even more than our science. We should have to abandon all understanding of the human world as meaningfully constituted, and so the one best hope of knowing ourselves.

Notes

CHAPTER 2

1. I have made this calculation from Murdock's ethnographic atlas (1967) by including only his categories of "patrilocal" (P), i.e., normal residence with or near male patrilineal kinsmen of the husband, and "patrilocal" preceded by temporary marital residence elsewhere (e.g., uP). If one were to add in the societies predominantly patrilocal but with significant deviations therefrom, the figures would reach 45 percent. I have not included "virilocality" (V), since Murdock defines this as to preclude patrilocal family formation. The sample in all calculations was n = 857.

2. Since the Kung Bushmen are one of the few exotic societies to which sociobiologists give much attention, it might be noted that the composition of Bushman bands is much like that of To'ambaita districts. Lorna Marshall has published the genealogies of four groups, chosen to exemplify "typical sizes of bands, typical families which compose the bands, and the typical pattern of relationships which bring persons, as individuals or in family groups, into residence together in bands" (1960, p. 338). Some 63 percent (37/49) of the married adults in Marshall's tables have some or all their primary kin (F, M, S, D, B or Z; $r = 1/2$) living in other bands. A good propor-

tion of these adults are in-marrying spouses—the exogamic line being third cousins—with principal economic obligations toward their affinal (rather than consanguineal) kin.

3. It deserves notice that the social fathering of other men's (biological) children is not restricted to extreme matrilineal systems or situations in which the "true" father is unknown. An early nineteenth-century observer of Tahitian society, system with a strong interest in bilateral descent, writes:

> Illegitimate children or those of adulterous unions were never the objects of baneful prejudice, having been welcomed as fully as all others. A husband may have been so jealously enraged by a wife's infidelity as to kill her; nevertheless, once children were born most husbands tended to treat them with care and affection even if they knew them to be not their own. And while one can find exceptions to this tendency, one can also cite cases in which the offspring of notoriously adulterous unions have been treated with lavish attention. It is fortunate that such was the case; for if a child's "legitimacy" had been viewed as we in our civilization view it, the unbridled sexual license which prevailed among these people would have resulted in an incalculable amount of misfortune and bad feelings (de Bovis, cited in Oliver 1974, vol. 2, p. 619).

4. I use "cognatic" and "bilateral" as synonyms, as the former is foreign to the nonanthropological ear. "Cognatic descent" refers to the tracing of ancestry indiscriminately through males or females, hence is to be distinguished from patrilineal descent (through males only) and matrilineal descent (through females only). From the point of view of the common ancestor, the cognatic group would include *all* his or her descendants, whereas patrilineal or matrilineal

descent excludes a moiety of such descendants. We shall see that cognatic descent cannot operate exclusively as a principle of group formation and solidarity, since where freedom is given to trace descent in any line, a person may belong to as many different groups as he has ancestors on any given generation. Residence in one of these groups is then the usual determination of de facto membership and solidarity, regardless of the ancestral connections to many other groups.

5. The principle of the "unity of siblings" refers to the fact that for social purposes vis-à-vis outside families, siblings act as a unit (cf. Radcliffe-Brown 1952). The further derivative principle of the "equivalence of siblings," or more specifically the equivalence of those of the same sex, implies that brothers belong in the same kinship class or category. Hence a man will be "son".to both his mother's husband and the latter's brother; both are "father." By the same logic, my father's father's brother's son is "father" also, and his son is therefore "brother" to me. This so-called merging of lineal and collateral relatives is technically called "classificatory kinship." We have already seen its operation in the discussion of Fijian kin categories.

6. As in many such cases purporting to quantify the reproductive effects of social behavior, the formula for kinship altruism in fact remains far from operational to Western science, let alone to ordinary social practice. Indeed, it does not appear that even the mathematics for kin selection among small sibling sets, as characterize the higher vertebrates, is yet available to Western science (cf. Levitt 1975).

7. One of the basic objectives of this entire exercise in the ethnography of kinship has been to show that the categories of "near" and "distant" vary independently of consanguineal distance and that these categories organize actual social practice. I have to underscore this basic point because sociobiologists, notably Alexander (1975), have taken the equally well-known tendency of economic reciprocity to vary in sociability with "kinship distance" as cultural evidence of biological "nepotism," hence as a proof of kin selection. One can see from the preceding discussion that this conclusion is based on an elementary misunderstanding of the ethnography. The kinship sectors of "near" and "distant," such as "own lineage" vs. "other lineage," upon which reciprocity is predicated, do not correspond to coefficient of relationship, so the evidence cited in support of kin selection (e.g., Sahlins 1965) in fact contradicts it (see also note 8).

8. John Tanner, a captive white man, was living as the son of an Ottawa Indian woman at Grand Portage in the early 1790s. The woman's husband had died, and Tanner and another man were doing the hunting, very unsuccessfully, when a man of the Muskogean tribe took the Ottawa people to his own lodge two days' travel distant. "He took us into his own lodge," Tanner relates, "and while we remained with him we wanted for nothing. . . . If anyone, who had at that time been of the family of Net-no-kwa [Tanner's Ottawa family], were now, after so many years, to meet one of the family of Pe-twaw-we-ninne [the Muskogean who had saved them]; he would call him 'brother,' and treat him as such" (Tanner 1956:24).

    Or, conversely, consider this recent ethnographic report from Easter Island:

Such a technique of treating kin as exchange partners whilst affirming that the exchanges are nothing more than sharing of resources appropriate to co-members of a family provides a rationale either for shedding unwanted kin, or, when expedient, for counting a genealogically remote cousin as closer kin than one of lesser degree. It results in a curious syllogism:

Family shares goods.

I will not share goods with you.

You will not share goods with me.

We are not family.

This attitude makes it easy for people to remove certain ancestors from their genealogies when it suits them simply by terminating exchange relations with other descendants (McCall 1976, p. 271).

CHAPTER 3

1. Or, to put the same in another economic perspective, Trivers has rediscovered the principle of consumer benefits. Following out this line of reasoning, Wilson reaches the interesting conclusion that money in human societies is a way of facilitating reciprocal altruism! "Money, as Talcott Parsons has been fond of pointing out, has no value in itself. It consists only of bits of metal and scraps of paper by which men pledge to surrender varying amounts of property and services upon demand; in other words, it is a quantification of reciprocal altruism" (Wilson 1975, p. 552). It must also follow that Euro-American capitalism, which has pushed the development of money to its greatest extent in human history, represents the apotheosis of altruism. One can see why the Left refuses to grant Wilson political immunity.

2. Since most avian species are monogamous, it must have been the fascination with Trivers's exploitative arguments for polygyny that led Wilson into

such an uncharacteristic speculative posture on this problem: "Monogamy is generally an evolutionarily derived condition. It occurs when exceptional selection pressures operate to equalize total parental investment and literally force pairs to establish sexual bonds. This principle is not compromised by the fact that the great majority of bird species are monogamous. Although polygamy in birds is in most cases a phylogenetically derived condition, the condition represents a tertiary shift back to the primitive vertebrate state. Monogamy in modern birds was almost certainly derived from polygamy in some distant avian or reptilian ancestor" (1975, p. 327). Wilson seems to be violating Lyell's principle of uniformatarianism; that is, in accounting for the origin of a phenomenon by a characteristic which cannot be found in the phenomenon as empirically known.

References

Alexander, Richard O.

    1974. The evolution of social behavior. *Annual Review of Ecology and Systematics* 5:325–38, 367–83.

    1975. The search for a general theory of behavior. *Behavioral Science* 20:77–100.

Ayres, Clarence.

    1944. *The theory of economic progress.* Chapel Hill: University of North Carolina Press.

Benveniste, Emile.

    1969. *Le vocabulaire des institutions indo-euro-péenes; vol. 1: Economie, parenté, société.* Paris: Editions de Minuit.

Berlin, Brent, and Paul Kay.

    1969. *Basic color terms.* Berkeley: University of California Press.

Boas, Franz.

    1965 [1911]. *Introduction to the handbook of American Indian languages.* (Published with J. W. Powell, *Indian linguistic families of America North of Mexico.*) Ed. P. Holder. Lincoln: University of Nebraska Press.

Brown, Paula, and H. C. Brookfield.

    1959–60. Chimbu land and society. *Oceania* 30: 1–75.

Cassirer, Ernst.

    1933. Le langage et la construction du monde des objets. *Journal de Psychologie Normale et Pathologique* 30:18–44.

Douglas, Mary.
  1973. Self-evidence. *Proceedings of the Royal Anthropological Institute of Great Britain and Ireland*, 1972, pp. 27–42.

Dumont, Louis.
  1970. *Homo Hierarchicus*. Chicago: University of Chicago Press.

Eco, Umberto.
  1976. *A theory of semiotics*. Bloomington: Indiana University Press.

Ellis, William.
  1969 [1842]. *Polynesian researches: Hawaii*. Rutland, Vermont: Tuttle.

Evans-Pritchard, E. E.
  1961. *Kinship and marriage among the Nuer*. Oxford: Clarendon Press.

Geertz, Clifford.
  1973. *The interpretation of cultures*. New York: Basic Books.

Ghiselin, M. T.
  1974. *The economy of nature and the evolution of sex*. Berkeley: University of California Press.

Hamilton, W. D.
  1964. The genetical theory of social behaviour. *Journal of Theoretical Biology* 12:12–45.
  1970. Selfish and spiteful behaviour in an evolutionary model. *Nature* 228:1218–20.
  1972. Altruism and related phenomena, mainly in social insects. *Annual Review of Ecology and Systematics* 3:193–232.

Hobbes, Thomas.
  1950 [1651]. *Leviathan*. New York: E. P. Dutton.

Hofstadter, Richard.
  1959. *Social Darwinism in American thought*. Revised edition. New York: Braziller.

Hogbin, H. Ian.
  1939. *Experiments in civilisation*. London: Routledge.

Hooper, Antony.
  1970a. 'Blood' and 'belly': Tahitian concepts of kinship and descent. In *Echanges et communications: Mélanges offerts à Claude Lévi-Strauss*, ed. J. Pouillon, and P. Maranda. The Hague: Mouton, vol. 1, pp. 306–20.
  1970b. Adoption in the Society Islands. In *Adoption in Eastern Oceania*, ed. V. Carroll. Honolulu: University of Hawaii Press, pp. 52–70.

Howard, Alan.
  1970. Traditional and modern adoption patterns in Hawaii. In *Adoption in Eastern Oceania*, ed. V. Carroll. Honolulu: University of Hawaii Press, pp. 21–51.

Langer, Susanne K.
  1971. The great shift: Instinct to intuition. In *Man and beast: Comparative social behavior*, ed. J. F. Eisenberg, and W. S. Dillon. Washington, D.C.: Smithsonian Institution Press, pp. 314–32.

Lévi-Strauss, Claude.
  1966. *The savage mind*. Chicago: University of Chicago Press.
  1969. *The elementary structures of kinship*. London: Eyre and Spottiswoode.

Levins, Richard.
  Unpublished. The limits of optimization.

Levitt, Paul R.
  1975. General kin selection models for genetic evolution of sib altruism in diploid and haplodiploid species. *Proc. Nat. Acad. Sciences* 79: 4531–35.

Macpherson, C. B.
  1962. *The political theory of possessive individualism*. London: Oxford University Press.

Malinowski, Bronislaw.
  1915. The natives of Mailu. *Transactions of the Royal Society of South Australia* 39:494–706.

1929.   *The sexual life of savages in North-Western Melanesia*. New York: Eugenics Publishing Co.

Malo, David.
1839.   Decrease of population. *Hawaiian Spectator* 2:121–30.

Marx, Karl, and Frederick Engels.
1965.   *The German ideology*. London: Lawrence and Wishart.

McCall, Grant.
1976.   *Reaction to disaster: Continuity and change in Rapanui social organisation*. Ph.D. dissertation, Australian National University.

Murdock, George P.
1967.   *Ethnographic atlas*. Pittsburgh: University of Pittsburgh Press.

Oliver, Douglas.
1974.   *Ancient Tahitian society*. 3 vols. Honolulu: University of Hawaii Press.

Ottino, Paul.
1972.   *Rangiroa: Parenté étendue, résidence et terres dans un atoll polynésien*. Paris: Editions Cujas.

Parsons, Talcott.
1968.   *The structure of social action*. 2 vols. New York: The Free Press.

Radcliffe-Brown, A. R.
1952.   *Structure and function in primitive society*. London: Cohen and West.

Reay, Marie.
1959.   *The Kuma*. Carlton: Melbourne University Press.

Sahlins, Marshall.
1962.   *Moala*. Ann Arbor: University of Michigan Press.
1965.   On the sociology of primitive exchange. In *The relevance of models for social anthro-*

pology, ed. M. Banton. London: Tavistock, pp. 139–236.

1976a. (in press) Colors and cultures. *Semiotica*.

1976b. (in press) *Culture and practical reason*. Chicago: University of Chicago Press.

Sartre, Jean-Paul.

1963. *Search for a method*. New York: Vintage Books.

Saussure, Ferdinand de.

1966 [1915]. *Course in general linguistics*. New York: McGraw-Hill.

Schmidt, Alfred.

1971. *The concept of nature in Marx*. London: NLB.

Schneider, David M.

1968. *American kinship: A cultural account*. Englewood Cliffs: Prentice-Hall.

1972. What is kinship all about? In *Kinship studies in the Morgan centennial year*, ed. P. Reining. Anthropological Society of Washington, pp. 32–63.

Schultz, T. W., ed.

1974. *Economics of the family*. Chicago: University of Chicago Press.

Sociobiology Study Group. "Science for the People."

1976 unpublished. Sociobiology: A new biological determinism.

Sumner, William Graham.

1934. *Essays of William Graham Sumner*. 2 vols. Ed. A. G. Keller, and M. R. Davie. New Haven: Yale University Press.

Tanner, John.

1956. *A narrative of the captivity and adventures of John Tanner*. Minneapolis: Ross and Haines.

Trivers, R. L.

1971. The evolution of reciprocal altruism. *Quarterly Review of Biology* 46:35–57.

1972. Parental investment and sexual selection.

In *Sexual selection and the descent of man, 1871–1971*, ed. B. Campbell. Chicago: Aldine, pp. 136–79.

1974.   Parent-offspring conflict. *American Zoologist* 14:249–64.

Wagner, Roy.

1967.   *The curse of Souw*. Chicago: University of Chicago Press.

West-Eberhard, M. J.

1975.   The evolution of social behavior by kin selection. *Quarterly Review of Biology* 50:1–34.

Williams, G. C.

1966.   *Adaptation and natural selection: A critique of some current evolutionary thought*. Princeton: Princeton University Press.

Wilson, Edward O.

1975.   *Sociobiology: The new synthesis*. Cambridge: Belknap Press of Harvard University Press.

1976.   Academic vigilantism and the political significance of sociobiology. *Bio Science* 26: 183, 187–90.

Wynne-Edwards, V. C.

1962.   *Animal dispersion in relation to social behaviour*. Edinburgh: Oliver and Boyd.